EACH BREATH
ALONG THE JOURNEY

A Collection of Short Stories and Essays
To Inspire You To "Live Your Best Life"

From the Author of:
"Waking Up: Lessons Learned Through
My Adventures With Life and Breast Cancer" and
"My Collective Soul: Things I Know
Without Knowing Why."

Anne Dennish

Library of Congress Control Number:		2019918666
ISBN:	Hardcover	978-1-7960-7114-6
	Softcover	978-1-7960-7113-9
	eBook	978-1-7960-7115-3

All photos found in this book are done by Anne Dennish
Author photos taken by Tim McGeough of EVN FLO Photography

Print information available on the last page.

Rev. date: 11/21/2019

To order additional copies of this book, contact:
Xlibris
1-888-795-4274
www.Xlibris.com
Orders@Xlibris.com
791099

Contents

CHAPTER THREE
"A Breath About Truth"

CHAPTER FOUR
"A Breath About Down Days"

CHAPTER FIVE
"A Breath About Being Positive"

CHAPTER SIX
"A Breath About Life Lessons"

CHAPTER SEVEN
"A Breath About Relationships"

CHAPTER EIGHT
"A Breath About Family"

CHAPTER NINE
"A Breath About Good Things"

With love and gratitude to the people who have been a part of my life. Some of you have stayed and some of you have gone, yet each one of you has given me reason to pause and breathe in the precious moments of my life. Each of you hold a special place in my heart and for that, I am forever grateful.

And for my children,
You are my heart and soul and have given me some of the most amazing breaths that a mother could ever take.

~Anne~

"Always be grateful for every day that you are gifted to have on this Earth and know that you are blessed with each breath along the journey."

~Anne Dennish~

PROLOGUE

I've come to see my life as a journey, one filled with a variety of adventures and life lessons. Each person along my travels has touched my life in one way or another. They've taught me a lesson, changed my perspective or challenged me to be the best version of myself.

Some have loved me and some have not. Some came into my life and stayed while others left my life as quickly as they had come into it. Some made me laugh and some made me cry, yet I believe with all my heart that each and every one of them was meant to cross my path at one point or another.

I've learned to look at every person, situation, and experience as a moment to pause and reflect, to observe and listen, to learn something from and be grateful.

And with each of those moments, I took a breath.

And every breath became a part of my journey.

And I will continue to learn and grow until the day I take my last breath.

~Anne~

CHAPTER ONE

"A Breath About Me"

"Once Upon A Time"

"Once upon a time there was a little girl who wanted to be a writer since the moment she learned to spell and so she began writing stories at a young age.

One day the little girl told her mother that she wanted to grow up to be a writer. Her mother said that it was a nice dream to have. The little girl didn't understand quite what that meant but she kept writing.

Time marched on and the little girl grew older, went to college and was still writing.

Then, the little girl got married and had children. She loved being a stay at home mom yet she still kept writing. She wrote little stories and poetry for her babies and made up silly songs to sing to them.

She wrote in her journal every day about her secret thoughts and feelings.

Then, the children started growing up and leaving the nest.

She thought about her "once upon a time" so many years ago.

She thought about all the people along her life journey that told her that wanting to be a writer was a nice dream and a fairy tale, but that real life isn't about doing what you love all the time and that most times dreams don't come true.

She believed them until one day when she stopped.

She stopped believing them and believing in herself.

She started to believe in fairy tales and dreams again. She started to believe in magic and she started to believe that everything and anything is possible.

It was on that day that she wrote her first book and had it published.

She knew at that moment that her "once upon a time" was a fairy tale that came true.

There was a happy ending and a beautiful beginning for her.

Once upon a time there was a little girl who wanted to be a writer.

The little girl grew up and became a writer and that wasn't the end.

It was just the beginning."

Everyone has a "once upon a time" that they believed in.

It's time to remember it again.

It's time to believe in it again.

After all, "once upon a time" does come true.

"The Life Of A Writer"

I love being a writer. It's crazy, enlightening, and therapeutic. It's living a life on fire with a passion for words, observing the world, for love, life, and the people in it. It's waking up at 3 in the morning and coming to life with a story in your head. It's nights of waking up during a good night's sleep with the next chapter writing itself in your mind. It's constant thinking, wondering and figuring it all out.

It's a 24 hour a day, 7 days a week job. The only days off are the ones in which you aren't physically writing on the computer or paper, but you're still writing in your head.

It's finding a story in every conversation you have, in every person you talk to during the course of a day, and in every social event you attend.

It's endless notebooks and journals of notes, titles, thoughts and new ideas.

It's always "remembering something so you never forget."

It's always analyzing a situation to figure out the lesson or the message.

It's always wondering "why" and "how" and "what if?"

It's always wondering about your past that led you to your present that will take you into your future.

It's always wondering what your dreams meant during the night and why certain thoughts enter your mind at the oddest of times during the day.

It's always wondering about the title of the next story, book, blog, or social media post.

It's a mind that never turns off, slows down, takes a break, or stops thinking.

It's a mind that's forever listening, wondering, seeing the endless possibilities in every minute of every day and in every person you speak to. It's a mind that is constantly taking in the energy of every experience and paying attention to every life lesson that comes along.

It's listening to different genres of music that pertain to your different moods: sad music for pity party days and upbeat music for when you're feeling great!

It's feeling all the emotions that life hands you and loving each and every one of them. You love the sad, the joy, the happy, and the heartache because a writer knows that every emotion is a gift, and each gift becomes the words to a beautiful story, poem or lyric.

Writers flourish under pressure and under pain. Our best writing comes from the deepest of pain. We hold onto it until we turn it into something beautiful and it's at that moment that we can finally let it go.

It's feeling the pain in the world and turning it into beautiful words of hope, faith and encouragement.

It's feeling the joy in the world and turning it into a motivational story of endless possibilities.

Writer's feel it all, accept it all, and love it all because no matter the emotion, negative or positive, sad or happy, we're able to embrace it, live it, feel it, learn from it and write about it.

It's then that we move on and not a moment sooner.

There are those in my life that tell me I hold onto things too long, to just "let it go," but as a writer, I can't. It's not in my nature nor is it in my soul. It's not how I'm wired or how I was born. It's not something I can change and I wouldn't want to try. It's who I am all wrapped in this body and soul, mind and heart.

Feeling pain is something I've grown accustomed to. Life happens and even pain and heartache happens to a writer. How else could we write the things that we do? Pleasure is born out of pain, happiness is born out of heartache, and joy is born out of sorrow. Why wouldn't we feel these emotions? It's our feelings that give us focus, clarity, and most importantly, it gives us the "words!"

Writer's are built on words.

We are great communicators.

We are intuitive, insightful and pay much more attention to detail than the average person. We listen, hear, process, and then we write and create.

We live everyday to its' fullest, no matter the emotions we're feeling. We don't see any emotion, good or bad, as a waste of time. We see it all as life, our life, and your life. We value all of it as precious time.

As for me, "when my heart speaks, I listen and then I write," and that's the truth.

My stories begin in my heart and soul and are cultivated through my tears and heartache. They are polished by my joy and happiness and are written by the words of my truth.

If the eyes are the window to the soul, my writing is the window into "me."

We writers are dreamers that many of the "real" world thinks is a waste of time.We can be viewed as obsessed and a little weird. They think we're constantly pursuing a dream we'll never catch, yet we believe differently. We believe in our dreams and in ourselves and are born out of this obsession to achieve the dreams, no matter the cost. Sure, we may come across to some as a bit weird, but that's because we know that what we dream, what we write and what we feel is our reality. It's the reality of a writer.

I love the life of being a writer. It's crazy, exhausting, painful, and happy at times, but to me, it's simply amazing.

I'm a writer, a dreamer and a poet.

I'm aware of my surroundings and all the people in it.

I'm a talker and a listener.

I'm your friend, your family and your lover.

I'm your mom and your mentor.

I'm all these things because…

I am Anne Dennish and I am a writer and for that, I'm grateful.

"More Than A Writer"

I've been writing since the day I could hold a pencil in my hand and learned to spell. Writing is as natural to me as breathing is. As a young child my stories were nothing more than a few sentences and a crayon drawing at the bottom of the page.

Throughout high school I could be found sitting on the beach like a Bohemian hippie, writing lyrics and poetry. There were countless nights during college that I spent writing in my notebook sitting against the wall in the hallway, a hot pot of coffee next to me, while the other students were sleeping.

I began keeping a journal of my thoughts and feelings during my marriage about being a wife and mother. I wrote poetry and journal entries which would later become short stories and those short stories became published books.

I was always writing something and still am.

A few years ago, whenever someone asked me what I did, I would say "I'm a mom." I was a Sunday School teacher, a soccer mom, PTA mom, Cub Scout leader and a Brownie leader. There was never a mention of "I'm a writer."

It's funny how you can write and write your whole life and never say that you were a writer.

That is, until my first book was published and even then I would say that "I write books."

It was one close high school friend, Rich, that said to me one day: "Why don't you say what you are? You're a writer. You're a published author. You're exactly what you wanted to be."

Wow! I never thought of myself as that, even though I was.

Why?

There's really no definitive answer as to "why" I never said it out loud or even thought of myself as that. I spent most of my life raising my kids, so to think of myself as someone other than that seemed like a foreign concept to me.

Yet, the truth of the matter is that I AM a writer. I AM a published author. I AM a lyricist.

In fact, I'm even more than that.

I'm a writer who uses her words in the hopes of making a difference in the life of another, and even in the world. I'm a writer who shares my personal stories with others so that they know they're not alone and that I went through tough times in my life, too. I'm a writer who wants to help others with their healing and inspire them to live their best life.

Writing is a part of my everyday life and as much of a part of me as breathing is.

Writing is my voice that I want to be heard.

Writing is my heart reaching out to love the world.

Writing is my soul that shares it passion.

Writing is my passion and my dream come true.

Writing is the one way I know how to reach people. It's my way of helping, sharing and making a difference in someone's life.

I AM more than a writer.

I'm a woman who's trying to make a positive difference in the world.

CHAPTER TWO

"A Breath About You"

"Everything Begins With You"

—◦❀◦—

Everything begins with you, yet there are moments that even I have to remind myself of that.

Those moments seem to come when we place more value on others than we do on ourselves and when that happens everything hits the fan!

We find ourselves seeing the true colors of friends and that they weren't who we thought they were. We find ourselves feeling betrayed, hurt and angry when that happens. We wonder why they couldn't be as loyal to us as we were to them, why they turned their back on us or why they crossed our boundaries of friendship. We wonder why a relationship we thought was perfect turns out to be anything but that. We wonder about a lot of things.

We wonder what happened, why things went the way they did, and if it all meant something more than what we thought. In other words, we want to know WHY it happened.

No one can control someone else, make them loyal to you, or make them love you.

We can only control ourselves.

That's a great power to have: the power to make decisions that are best for YOU!

You see, somewhere along your journey in life you lost sight of how valuable you are.

You valued someone else so much that you forgot to value yourself.

If you can't see how valuable you are, how do you expect anyone else to see it?

It all begins with you.

Walk away from those who bring you down. Wish them love and light, be grateful for the lessons your experience with them taught you, and let them go.

Let go of the negative people you've allowed in your bubble and make room for the positive people that are meant to come in.

Know your value.

Know your worth.

Know that you don't deserve anything less than that.

"How Did I Get Here?"

My friend called me one morning and asked me this question: "Don't you ever ask yourself how you got here? Don't you wonder how you got to this place in your life?"

I told him I already knew how I got "here." It was because of a "series of unfortunate events," which I look at as a "series of fortunate events" because they've enabled me to become the person that I am today.

You see, I was standing at a cross road during each of those "unfortunate events," a crossroad in which I could go one way or the other. I chose the right path most of the time and the times that I didn't I went through another "unfortunate event" and was given another chance to choose the right path.

The "right path" was the one of recovery, healing, and at times, of survival.

The "wrong path" was the one of repeating the same patterns and mistakes, and the one which gave me another chance to remember the life lesson that I had forgotten.

In the end, each path you choose is the one that will get you to "here." I believe that all the experiences we go through in life were meant to happen and are what brought us to where we are now. You have a choice to take those "series of unfortunate events" and turn them into something positive. You have a choice to let those events take you out and keep you down, yet you also have a choice to let them teach you, heal you, and move you forward into a different and better life. It's your choice to let the "unfortunate events" keep you down or to use them to raise you up into becoming your best sense of self.

I've gone through divorce, abuse and breast cancer.

I survived them all and with that survival I'm able to share all of my experiences of how I got through them with others.

In the end, all those "unfortunate events" happened to me to bring me to "here." They've made me who I am today. They've enabled me to stay true to my dreams so that I can keep trying to make a positive difference in the life of another and in this world.

"Each path you've chosen in life has gotten you to where you are now and it's exactly where you're supposed to be."

"Right Where You Belong"

"Sometimes life takes us on an unexpected turn, taking us on the journey of a lifetime. We may not end up where we had dreamed, but we will always end of where we belong."

I wrote this quote years ago and for good reason: my life didn't go as I had hoped, planned or dreamed and I had to change my perspective on it. I had to learn to accept that the Universe had other plans in place for me which were different than mine. I had to accept that perhaps, in this grand scheme of life, the Universe puts us all in the place we belong in at that time in our life.

Life certainly does take an unexpected turn at times. We go along living our life day by day thinking that it will always be like that, until it isn't. We're blindsided that this peaceful life we're living twists and turns into something other than what we had wanted. We wonder why certain things happen to us, why the people we love stopped loving us or how friends or family showed us their true colors and let us see that they never were the people we thought they were.

We wonder.

I wonder.

Then I stop wondering.

I stop because I believe that everything happens for a reason and happens as it should, when it should and how it should.

I remind myself that I may not be where I had dreamed, but I'm exactly where I belong at this time in my life.

Life is always changing and the path along the journey can throw us for a loop, sending us into a tailspin. Take a breath, accept that whatever has happened is a life lesson to move you forward and trust that the journey is leading you to the beautiful life you deserve.

Sometimes it's the place in our life that we never dreamed of being in that turns out to be exactly where we were meant to be.

"Never Forget How Far You've Come"

The older we get, the more experiences we have under our belts yet there are times we forget how far we've come in this life journey.

All of us go through rough days and tough times, no matter our age. It's those moments of wondering how in the world we're going to make it through, how we're going to get past this difficult experience, how we're going to find strength in a soul that is exhausted.

Yet, we do and do you know how?

It's by remembering that you made it through.

You need to remember what you've already gone through and that you made it through, albeit sometimes by the skin of your teeth. You made it through stronger, different, and better. You did what you had to do to get through. You need to remember those times when you thought you'd never make it, because you did. Give yourself credit that you found the strength and the will to get through something difficult and come out on the other side even better.

Never forget how far you've come and the lessons you learned. Never forget that some of those difficult times taught you the most important lessons you needed to know so that you could live a better life.

Never forget when you were feeling as if you'd never make it through, and remember the feeling of how good you felt when you did.

You made it through another day, slept through another night and woke up to a new day in the morning.

A new day with no mistakes in it.

A new day to do it all differently than the day before.

A new day to change your life.

A new day to change your perspective.

A new day to live your best life.

A new day to be excited over all the endless possibilities it has to offer you.

That day is a very good day.

Life will always throw a challenge or two our way, yet it's so important to remember that we've been through difficult times before and we made it through.

"Never forget how far you've come."

Remember that.

Always remember that.

Celebrate the challenges you've made it through and be grateful for just how far you've come.

"What You Seek"

"Everything you seek is seeking you." ~Rumi~

Everything you want in your life can be found within you. It's there but sometimes you aren't able to see the dream turned into a reality or the opportunity that is right within your grasp. You may not be able to see this for different reasons: fatigue, illness, stress, drama, or sadness.

The key is to know that they are reasons and should not be turned into excuses.

If you're tired, then be sure to get a good night's sleep.

If you don't feel well, then do what you have to do to feel better.

If you're dealing with stress, then do what you can to figure out why and how to get rid of it.

You see, everything we seek in our life is also seeking us. We sometimes get so caught up in things that we have no control over that we lose our balance. Our health suffers, our sleep is disrupted, or our mood turns dark. We need to be aware of the situations around us that are taking up too much of our time. Does the stress you're feeling or the drama that you're part of belong to you or someone else? If it's yours then you need to do what it takes to handle the stress and get rid of the drama. If it's someone else's then you need to let it be their stress, not yours, and walk away.

We can only control ourselves and when we do so in a positive way, less negative stuff will be around us. Love yourself first, take care of yourself as well as you take care of others, respect yourself, know yourself, and above all else, don't give more of your precious time away to other people than you would give to yourself.

"Remember This: It's Not "Me First," It's "Me Too!"

It's when you do those things that you will soon find your life changing in the way that you want it to. Doors begin opening that you thought were closed, new opportunities present themselves in amazing ways and you suddenly feel a peace that you couldn't have imagined.

Everything you want is within your arms' reach. Reach out, wrap your arms around it, and hold tight to it. It's all there within you.

Take care of yourself so that you can see it.

Be well rested so that you can find it.

Keep your mind and heart open so that you can accept it.

"Your Imperfections Make You Beautiful"

I believe that it's important to be mindful of keeping my words and my thoughts positive. Words have a powerful impact on both ourselves and others, whether positive or negative. We feel the words that we say and that are said to us, which is why positivity shines so bright and negativity hides in darkness.

No one is perfect, least of all me, but I would rather lift someone up with positive words than bring them down by telling them their faults. In fact, if you want to see someone become the awesome person they truly are, speak kindly to them, tell them their strengths, how you feel about them, and focus on the good things about them, not the negative.

Our imperfections make us beautiful. Our flaws make us flavorful. Our quirks make us memorable.

I've raised five children and believe me, there have been times that they've done things that have bothered me. I love them with all my heart and for who they are, yet I would rather tell them what I love about them and what their strengths are rather than tell them their faults, such as "you left the wet towel on the floor again, why don't you put the cap on the toothpaste" and so on.

As the children have grown, I have as well. I chose to pick my battles. I try and lift everyone in my life up. I try never to pick at the small things because there are so many more big and wonderful things about them. It's those same silly things that bother us that we'll miss one day.

I can promise you that when you continually point out someone's faults to them, they're going to shut down because what you're telling them is that you don't accept them for who they are and that all you see are their faults. You can tell them that you love them but they won't feel it because all you do is pick at what you don't like about them rather than telling them what you do.

If you're consistently looking for perfection from the people that you surround yourself with, then you'll be disappointed. We're human beings and we're not meant to be perfect, so if all you see in someone is "imperfection," then do them a favor and leave them be. Most of us know our shortcomings and don't need to be reminded of them from someone else. It only hurts their heart and bruises their self-esteem.

Ask yourself these questions: "How would you feel if the people you love were constantly picking at you and telling you what was wrong with you and how you should change?" Would you begin to shut down? Would you stop caring? Would you feel badly because someone you care about was talking down to you?"

Think about it. Are you lifting others up by treating them with kindness and positive words or are you beating them down by being cruel and using negative words?

It's simple: treat the people in your life the way you want to be treated.

Pick your battles, accept the people you love for who they are, not who you want them to be, and lift them up with positive words because the negative words you speak to them will bring them down and will only hurt you as well in the end.

See the good and stop seeing the bad.

Pick your battles, my friends, please pick your battles.

"Value"

Do you value the people in your life? Do you appreciate them? Do you tell them how much they mean to you? Do you let them know how grateful you are for them and all that they do for you? Do you support them? Do you treat them with respect? Do you love them?

I'm sure you said "yes" to all or most of those, but the real question here is this: "Do they treat you the same?"

Some of you may say "no" to that question and if you did, you need to ask yourself this next question: "Why do you let them?"

Don't you see your own value, your own worth?

The right person/people will see it as well, and if they don't, then the cold hard truth is that they're using you for their own benefit and maybe, just maybe, they don't see any value in you at all.

"The person who doesn't value you is not your person."

Love yourself enough to know what you deserve and what you don't.

Love yourself enough to know who your person is and isn't.

Love yourself enough to know just how valuable and amazing you are.

It's when you can do that you'll find that the people that surround you ARE your people.

"A To-Do List For You!"

I woke up this morning with gratitude for another day. I made my first cup of coffee and sat on my front porch to watch the sunrise. It was peaceful and as I was sitting there watching the burnt orange skies of the sunrise, I was writing my "to-do list" for the day. In fact, I write a list everyday! The truth is, I have many of those lists cluttering my desk, yet not one of them is ever completely checked off as "DONE!"

I began to think about "why" the list doesn't get done. Some days I'm tired or my allergies have gotten the best of me. Some days I lack the motivation and energy to get those things done. Some days I allow situations that aren't my problem or concern to distract me.

So, I made a decision that there will be no more of that nonsense!

This morning a new idea was born in this already over-crowded mind of mine: "What about making a to-do list for ME?" Why not make a list of things I want to do or need to do to stay focused and balanced, feel healthier, and have more energy to accomplish the tasks on the other list?

I decided that instead of writing yet another "to-d0 list" filled with tasks such as "make a doctors appointment, go to the post office, run to the food store, or reschedule the dentist," I was going to write a "to-do list" for me and I think it's a good thing for all of us to do.

Write a list of things that are just for YOU! It could begin with morning coffee and meditation, a 20 minute daily walk, yoga, healthier eating, or changing habits that don't enable you to live your best life.

Life gets busy and we may find ourselves distracted by outside influences that are not our concern. We lose sight of taking care of ourselves. I know that in order to accomplish anything in my life, let alone my day, I need to feel whole, healthy, focused and balanced.

I've decided to begin each new week in a different way and that's with writing a "to-do list" for me.

What's on YOUR "to-do list?" Decide what you need to do for YOURSELF to live your best life.

"Love Yourself Enough To Make The Time"

I had an insanely busy week a few months ago. I went to dinner with good friends on Friday, took a road trip to Virginia on Saturday for my nephew's graduation party, then back home on Sunday night. I had an early eye doctor appointment on Monday morning and the dentist on Tuesday. I was happy to wake up on Wednesday knowing that I had nothing scheduled.

Don't get me wrong, that week was wonderful but every so often, and sometimes more often than not, we all have to slow down and take time for ourselves. We need to make the time to simply enjoy the beauty that surrounds us. We need to make the time to relax, to breathe, to clear our minds of all the clutter that can build up in it. We need to nourish our body and our soul.

So often I hear people say "I just can't seem to find the time to do this or do that." I'm here to tell you that while that may be a true statement, the reality is that we don't "find the time," we have to love ourselves enough to "make the time."

What do you need to "make the time for?"

I'm making the time to work on another new book, make a few phone calls to friends, and the most important thing I'm doing today is to sit outside in nature and enjoy a day at the Shore.

"Make the time" today and everyday for something that helps you to live your best life and be your best sense of self.

Love yourself enough to "make the time" for YOU.

"Unbecoming"

There are times we feel frustrated at where our life is at this very moment. We thought we'd be in a better place financially or that our career would have skyrocketed by now. We thought we'd stop attracting the same type of people into our circle or that we'd be in a place which held more peace than stress.

It's part of the journey.

Yet, think about this: maybe the journey isn't going the way we want because we're being the person everyone else wants us to be, not the person we were meant to be or want to be.

We have to be our authentic selves, no matter what anyone else wants us to be.

Our journey can only be what we want it to be when we stand in our truth and be who are meant to be.

Sometimes "the journey isn't about becoming anything, it's about unbecoming everything that isn't really you, so you can be who you were meant to be in the first place." ~Paul Coelho~

Be who you are.

Be your authentic self.

Be awesome.

"A Little Bit of Everything"

One of my favorite songs is "Little Bit of Everything" by Keith Urban. It's a great song about wanting the smallest of things in life that mean the most, and it started me thinking: "I just want a little bit of everything, too."

I want a little bit of love.

I want a little bit of joy and happiness.

I want a little bit of compassion, respect and understanding.

I want a little bit of laughter and fun.

I want a little bit of someone who cherishes me and makes me a priority.

I want a "little bit of everything."

Then I stopped myself and changed my thinking.

I don't want a little bit of all those things.

I want a lot of all those things.

I'm not going to settle for "a little bit of everything" when I know life holds "a lot of everything" for me.

In order for "a lot of everything" to come into my life, I have to be sure to love myself enough to know that I deserve a lot more than a little bit.

So do you.

"The What and The Why"

"What's" happened to you in your life isn't as important as "why" it happened.

We all experience some difficult situations in our life and I've come to accept and understand that the "what" that's happened to me isn't as important as the "why" it did.

We're so quick to blame others for our difficult times, yet we have a hand in those situations as well. Perhaps we aren't being our authentic self or standing in our truth to those around us. Maybe we change "who" we are according to the people we are around at a particular moment. I can tell you that I've learned that I am in control of what I allow to happen to me and it's up to me to set healthy boundaries for my highest good, and that's not always so easy to do.

I had breast cancer and it can't always be prevented, yet I could have had a mammogram sooner than I did. I went 5 years without one and only had one done when I found my tumor. So, while this "what" may have been destined to happen to me, the "why" it happened when it did was because I wasn't loving myself enough to get that mammogram every year like I should have. I know better now.

We've all lived through relationships at one time or another in our life that didn't work out, whether it was an ending to a marriage, love affair or friendship. The "what" that caused an ending to these relationships isn't as important as the "why" it happened. It happened because I was allowing those people to treat me in a way I didn't deserve and what you allow will continue. It continued for me until I realized I deserved better and decided to stop it.

I've lived through emotional, verbal and physical abuse. It went on for years until I finally put an end to it. "What" was said and done to me isn't as important as "why" it was done to me. It happened because I let it happen. I wasn't as strong as I am now, my self-esteem was non-existent, and I blamed myself for causing all those things that were said and done to me then. I was at the bottom and when I finally decided that enough was enough, I pulled myself up off the floor and began to see clearly of the "why" it happened. I began to get stronger day by day and set up boundaries that were never again to be crossed by anyone, and if they were, I certainly recognized it sooner. It happened because I let it, not because I deserved it. It was yet another life lesson for me to learn.

You have to love yourself, respect yourself, and know that you don't deserve to be treated badly by anyone, especially by yourself. Let's face it, we're all masters of self-sabotage at times and we can hurt ourselves better than the person who is hurting us, but that's not the way it should be.

It's time all of us, myself included, stop focusing on the "what" that happened to us and start looking deep within ourselves to see our truth of the "why" it happened.

It's then that we learn, grow and move forward into the life we want and deserve.

"TIME TO SHIFT"

When you change your thinking from "why is this happening to me" with "what is this trying to teach me," everything in your life shifts.

So often we find ourselves in situations that upset us and our first thought is always "why is this happening to me?"

The answer is always the same: "Life is trying to teach you something about yourself."

Now the work begins. You need to look long and hard at the situation and think about how and why it happened.

Did someone say something hurtful to you? Did someone make you cry? Did someone point a finger of blame at your for being who you are?

If the answer to any of these questions is "yes" then you need to still your mind, take a deep breath and ask yourself "why?"

The answer to this is always the same: "Because you allowed it."

You let them treat you in a way that you didn't deserve and what you allow will continue.

It always does and that's what the situation is about.

It's not randomly happening TO YOU, it's happening FOR YOU. The Universe is trying to teach you a life lesson. It's asking you the tough question: "Why would you let someone treat you like that?"

Most of us don't know how to answer that except to make excuses for the other person's bad behavior. It's having a false hope that it won't happen again and that they really didn't mean it. It's a false hope of believing that the person will change. It's a false hope that they'll say they're sorry and mean it.

I've been in that position in this lifetime more times than I can count, but I've grown as a person, become stronger, and believe that those moments of pain and heartache were because I allowed someone to treat me badly. question.

I've come to understand that people who treat you badly or abuse you do so because you allow them to get away with. There's a problem with THEM, not YOU. There are many reasons that people treat someone badly and most times it's because of their insecurities, jealousies, low self-esteem and lack of control in their own life. They have a choice to change for the better, but it has to be THEIR choice. You can't force another to change.

You have to ask yourself the question: "Why did I allow someone to treat me so badly?"

Only you can answer the question of why you let it happen.

Only you can figure out the lesson it was trying to teach you.

Only you can change yourself. You can continue to allow others to treat you badly or can begin to demand respect from them.

Most often times those situations happen to remind us that we're important, that we count, and that we are valuable.

They happen to remind us to love ourselves more, be kind to ourselves and respect ourselves.

They happen to remind us that we should always be kind and if we can't be kind, then we should be quiet. They remind us that no one should treat another human being badly, because there is no excuse or reason for the bad behavior. They remind us that we all have a heart and soul that can be easily broken, and it takes time and effort for the healing to begin.

The healing begins with YOU when you understand the lesson that life hit you with.

Only you can change the situation and only you can stop allowing those experiences to happen.

Stop focusing your energy on thinking about "why this is happening to you" and begin to shift your focus and energy to "what is this trying to teach me?"

The moment you can do that is the moment that everything shifts.

"Time For A Change"

I'm ready for a change, are you? I don't know if it's the time of year, the change of the seasons, the cold I've had for two weeks or simply "restless soul syndrome," but I know I need a change.

The holiday rush is beginning and the house needs to be decorated. The boys and I are recuperating slowly from colds and the weather jumps from torrential downpours to below freezing temperatures. It's no wonder I'm feeling restless.

I'm writing a new book and trying to figure out how I can find public speaking platforms so that my voice can be heard, not just read off social media or in one of my books. I'm in the process of making decisions for a healthier lifestyle for my family and me, one which entails cleaner eating and more exercise.

It's no wonder I have "restless soul syndrome."

I know the holiday time of year can be overwhelming. There's so much to be done and so little time to do it in, yet if there's one thing I always have to remind myself, it's this: "Stop, breathe, relax and remember that it won't be like this forever, just for today."

It so is important to remember that, not just at the holidays, but everyday.

So, in the midst of this feeling of the need for change, I'm making a list of what I want to change, of things I want to do, and of how to turn some of my dreams into a reality.

I'm always telling people that "everything begins with you," and that's true, but do you know what else is true? That the changes you want to see in your life begin with you as well.

Embrace that feeling of needing a change and embrace that feeling of "restless soul syndrome."

After all, it's your intuition saying to you that it's time for a new adventure, another chapter, and a new beginning, ones that will make your life even better.

So next time you're feeling restless, listen to your soul.

"And Now I'll Do What's Best For Me"

You can't change someone or save them. You can only change and save yourself. It's a tough one for me to remember sometimes because I want to help everyone have a good life. I want everyone to feel better. I want everyone to have healthy relationships. I want everyone to feel peace.

Did you notice that I didn't include myself in that?

I noticed that, too.

So, now I'm going to "change" that by saying it the way I should have: "I want to have a good life. I want to feel better. I want a healthy relationship, and I want to feel peace."

Much better.

All too often we forget that everything we want in life begins with us.

All too often we focus our time and energy on people that wouldn't do the same for us.

All too often we love others more than they love us and more than we love ourselves.

All too often we're taken for granted when we should be appreciated.

Let's change all that right now.

Repeat after me: "And now I'll do what's best for ME!"

You're not being selfish by doing what's best for you, you're being self-less. You're loving yourself. You're taking care of yourself and you're taking control of your life.

You're doing what's best for YOU!

"Be The Positive Change"

I've found myself in conversations with people who seem to ask me the same question: how do I make my life better, happier, more positive?

My answer is always the same: "you have to be the positive change you want to be and see."

However, what they fail to realize is that the positive change is more than a state of mind, it's a state of being. It's how you treat people and what type of vibes you put out into the world. It's your perspective and your attitude. It's accepting the ups and downs that life hands you and learning the lessons from them.

You can't expect your life to change unless you're willing to make the changes you want to see.

How do you treat people? Are you kind and considerate? Do you judge them based on the opinions of others or do you form your own opinion by getting to know them personally? Do you speak nicely to people or do you verbally abuse them?

What type of vibes are you putting out into the world? Are you a positive person or a negative person? Are you trying to bring out the best in others or just the stress in them? Are you trying to make a positive impact on the world or expecting the world to make one on you?

Are you close minded or do you allow your mind to be open to see another side of a situation or person? Do you have a mind of your own or do you have a mind that someone told you to have? When challenged by someone who has a different perspective than you, are you willing to listen to their thoughts or do you believe that yours are always right?

Do you have a positive attitude when faced with a difficult situation or do you feel hopeless and negative? Are you always saying "why me" or accepting "why not me?" Is your mind open to understand that it's through difficult times that we learn valuable life lessons, ones that teach us a different way to be so that we don't go through them again?

I believe that we can ALL be the positive change we want to see in this world and I also believe that sometimes our best efforts to do this aren't always well received by some people. Rest assured, it's not your fault, it's theirs. Some people choose to live their lives with drama and stress, jealousy and insecurity, rather than change their life of negativity into one of positivity.

It's not your job to fix them or save them. The responsibility of doing that is on them, yet what you can do is be all those positive changes you want to see in the world. Some people will love you for it, and some will hate you for it, but don't ever stop being that positive person because of their behavior. Be you. Be your best you. Let your light shine in this world and those that are in the darkness will either see the light or stay where they are.

You can't expect to talk down to someone, verbally abuse someone, judge someone, ignore someone or break the heart and soul of someone without a reaction.

You can say all the right words to someone but if you don't have the actions to back them up they'll never be truth. It's the actions that make the words true.

Words are the most powerful thing in the world, and I don't say that just because I'm a writer, I say it because it's true.

If you say hurtful things to someone they will remember those words long after you apologized for saying them.

If you break someone's heart they're going to remember how you broke it more than how you tried to fix it.

If you treat someone badly they will remember that feeling forever.

I know a lot of good people that I'm blessed to have in my life. There have been a few that were not good people cross my path, but I'm grateful for the lessons that their behavior taught me.

Be the change you want to see in your life, your relationships and your heart. Be the person who makes a positive impact on someone's life. Be the one who makes a difference in the world.

Remember, if you want to see a positive change in your life you must be willing to be that positive change.

You can do it.

We all can.

All of us have the choice to "be the positive change."

"Express Yourself"

The only way you're going to know who should and shouldn't be in your life is by standing in your truth.

Be who you really are, not the person that you think someone wants you to be.

Know that you don't have to agree with the opinions of others just because you want to fit in.

Understand that you are not everyone's "cup of tea," and some people aren't yours either.

Never assume that someone knows what you're thinking or feeling.

That's what "standing in your truth" is all about.

It's being your complete, authentic self to the people you meet, because when you hide who you truly are, you run the risk of attracting the wrong people into your life. They may like you for who you pretend to be, but is that what you want? I know I don't.

I don't change to fit the person I'm with. I'm a "what you see is what you get" kind of girl. You have to be your authentic self in order to have the right people in your life.

That's how you surround yourself with "like-minded" people, ones who are positive, have your back, and lift you up instead of bringing you down. You want people who understand your differences and accept you for who you are, the people who acknowledge your successes and keep you motivated to turn your dreams into a reality, and the people who love you for who you are, not for who they want you to be.

Don't silence your voice to make someone else happy, to prevent a disagreement, or to keep things calm.

The right people will embrace your voice and your truth.

The right people will love you for who you are.

The right people won't try to change you.

The right people will never try to silence your voice because they know that your voice is your truth.

Your voice is "you."

Be you.

"Finding Your Old Bucket List"

I had been trying to make good use of my time while my body was slowly recovering from a virus, so I began going through closets, papers and old files. It's amazing what a person can find when you start doing that.

I had to laugh at an old "Bucket List" I found from 2011. Well, maybe not laugh, but it sure made me remember. It brought me back to that time in my life over 8 years ago. The funny thing is that I actually have done a few things on that list years after I wrote them.

"Try a day as a blonde." Check!

"Drive in a convertible someplace exciting." Check!

"Write about my life so that my kids will really know me as someone other than their mother." Check!

"Reach out to someone going through a similar situation that I had so that they don't feel alone." Check!

"Speak in front of an audience and be able to say something to them that makes a difference in their lives." Check!

"Go on a photo shoot." Check!

It's interesting that I had written those goals so long ago and did them years later without a thought that they had ever been on a list. It's quite an eye opener to realize that while I've changed throughout the years, I hadn't changed what I wanted to do in this life of mine: make a difference in someone's life and in the world.

There's some things on that list that are yet to be done and new things I want to add to it.

As I continue the decluttering and purging of my house, I'm going to write a new "Bucket List" and tuck that away with my papers.

I'm hoping that in another 8 years from now I'll come across it and realize that I've checked off everything on it.

"Go Barefoot"

Imagine for a moment that you met the perfect person and find yourself in the best relationship of your life. Imagine that you find a group of friends that are just like you and land the job of a lifetime. Imagine that your kids are all doing great and everyone in your family is getting along. Imagine that you are the happiest you've ever been in your life.

Have you been there? Can you imagine how great it feels to have all that you want?

We all can and we've all been there.

Sometimes when we get there in life we get nervous and feel afraid that all this great stuff in our life is going to be taken away.

In other words, when life is all that we want it to be we find ourselves "waiting for the other shoe to drop."

After all, life isn't always easy and when it seems as if it is, we sometimes find ourselves spending more time feeling nervous of losing it than we do of spending more time enjoying it.

Trust me, even I find myself so happy sometimes that I can't help but get a bit nervous it will be taken away.

So, I decided that when those moments of "waiting for the other shoe to drop" find their way into my mindset, I change it and tell myself to "go barefoot!"

It's a silly and simple concept, but our mind is a powerful tool and the more positive we keep our thoughts, the more positive things will come into our life.

I know this to be true.

Embrace the person who is the love of your life, be happy about the best job you've ever had and be grateful for the happiness you feel.

Don't let fear get in the way of any of that and the next time you find yourself waiting for "the other shoe to drop," kick them off and "GO BAREFOOT!"

"When The Universe Opens A Door"

The Universe is always hard at work for us, opening doors that we never knew needed opening and closing those that we weren't able to close ourselves. More often than not, we don't even realize that it's happening, but it is. Things happen for our Highest Good, to help us move forward into living our best life every day, which is why it's so important to pay attention to the signs.

It's important that when a door we didn't expect to open suddenly does, we need to go through it. The truth is, when doors are opened up for us they don't stay open forever. We need to act in that moment to take a leap of faith and walk through it, otherwise an opportunity that can open many more doors for us will be missed.

I realized that it had been happening in my life. Suddenly, I began to think of all the things that have happened in my busy life and could see what was happening: the Universe was opening doors for me. It was offering me opportunities which I hadn't even asked for and putting "like-minded" people in my path.

All of us can get so busy with day to day life that we forget to pay attention to what's going on around us. We miss opportunities, we're blind to the signs, and we run on adrenaline instead of intuition.

I remembered that everything happens as it should, how it should and when it should. I could see all the gifts that were showing up in my life, all the doors that were beginning to open, and all the opportunities being given to me.

I know that doors don't always open when we need them to and I'm certainly not going to take the doors that open for me for granted.

I'm taking yet another leap of faith and allowing all these open doors to lead me to where I need to be and to where I'm supposed to be.

I'm incredibly grateful to the Universe for paying attention to ME!

Pay attention to the signs that are all around you.

Believe in your dreams, believe in yourself, and be brave enough to take a leap of faith.

"When a door opens for you, take a leap of faith and walk through and if the door you want doesn't open, it's not your door."

Trust the journey.

CHAPTER THREE

"A Breath About Truth"

"STANDING IN YOUR TRUTH"

We're never too old to learn something new about ourselves and I recently learned something so valuable about myself that it is life changing and will definitely help me in living my best life more than I had been.

I write and speak often about "fear," and that nothing good can come from it. I talk about standing in your truth and using your voice in a kind, respectful way to express that truth. I talk about the importance of taking the time to understand any fear you may be facing and share my experiences of how I've managed to do that.

My most recent "waking up moment" was that I realized I had been carrying a "fear" which I wasn't even aware of. Sometimes a situation happens in your life that brings a life lesson to you, one that gives you an opportunity to see something in yourself that you hadn't been able to see before.

I see it now and I want to share it with you.

I love and value the people in my life and I would never want to lose them, and that's a human and normal way to feel, but I realized that in not wanting to lose them I've become "fearful" of losing them. I suddenly began to see that I wasn't standing in my truth as much as I should have or saying what I needed to say to them because I didn't want to anger or hurt them. I was under the impression that if I did that, they'd leave my life, and that is so not the way to be with anyone in your life: friend, family member, partner or spouse.

I realized that this was a fear that should never have been part of who I am because in the end, anyone who would leave my life because of who I am and what I say didn't really value me at all. And that is the truth. It's my truth now and I'm working on releasing this fear that was buried within me for much of my life.

We're all humans who, at times, don't even understand why we act the way we do or feel the way we do, yet once we address these underlying issues of our own and understand the "why" behind them, we release them. It's then that we begin to grow into our best sense of self. We begin the journey of healing, of recovery and the road to truly "living our best life."

This was quite a life lesson for me to learn but such an important one. I'm continuing on the path of standing in my truth and using my voice to express it. It's time to take this fear that had been buried inside of me for so long, wish it love and light, send it on its way. After all, the bigger fear in this picture is losing myself and that's not something I want to happen, and neither should you.

"Don't be afraid of losing someone by standing in your truth. Be afraid of losing yourself if you don't."

"Who Are You Letting Into Your Bubble?"

My friend, Peg, called me the other day to ask my opinion about a situation. She was feeling hurt over someone crossing her boundaries and in seeing the truth of them. She realized that who she thought they were turned out to have not been who they truly were. She asked me how to get past that emotion of feeling hurt and betrayed.

I thought about it for a moment and came up with this analogy, one which I hope helps everyone.

Picture your life as a bubble and you're in the center. Let's say you're only allowed 10 people inside of it with you. Picture those 10 people sitting in the chairs. Look around. Take a long, hard look to see which ones bring out the best in you and which ones bring out the stress in you. If the chairs in your bubble are filled with 6 positive people and 4 negative, then there aren't any seats left for other positive people to come in. Your bubble is full to capacity, and it's filled with negative and positive people.

I can't tell anyone enough that it is your decision of who you allow in your bubble and you should always love yourself enough to want to surround yourself with positive people. They are the types of people who are loyal to you, have your back, love and respect you, lift you up, support you, and more importantly, are honest with you. You want to keep the energy in your bubble as positive as possible, because negativity breeds negativity and you don't want an epidemic of that inside!

When you realize that there are some negative people in your bubble and you want more positive people taking their place, do the math. You need to end your relationships with the negative people, wish them love and light, be grateful for the lessons they taught you, and move forward. It's not always easy to let go of certain people, yet when you do, you've just opened a few more seats up in your bubble and have made room for the positive people to come in.

We all find ourselves in this situation now and again, yet it's important to understand that these experiences happen to teach us a lesson about ourselves. Each of us has the control of who we allow in our bubble and each of us had a choice of keeping it positive or allowing the negative to take up residence.

Who do you have in your bubble? Is the energy inside of your bubble feeling positive? Are there more negative than positive people in there with you?

Only you know the answer to those questions and only you can choose what's best for you.

Think about it.

The decision is yours.

After all, it's your life and your bubble.

"Drawing A Line In The Sand"

Boundaries. I know about them, write about them, and understand their purpose. Yet, there are times that I find myself allowing MY boundaries to be crossed, and I want to share a particular experience of mine with you.

It happened without warning, yet it happened. I should have known that the feelings I was having over the course of a few months were my own fault. I had healthy boundaries set, yet I allowed them to be crossed.

I don't know if I was more angry at myself for allowing it to happen or if I was more upset with the person who crossed them. I was open and honest about my boundaries with them, yet somehow they got lost in the everyday business of life and relationships.

The truth is that I sometimes have a hard time saying "no" and learning to do this, especially when it's for my best interest, is a work in progress. I don't like confrontation and don't want to hurt someone's feelings, especially when it's someone I love, yet I missed one very important piece to this puzzle: "Why did I allow MY feelings to be hurt and why was I more concerned over someone I love when I should have been loving myself just the same?"

There it was, a slap of reality. Yes, it was another "waking up" moment for me and one that I wasn't too fond of, but I knew I needed to face it. I allowed boundaries to be crossed that upset me, hurt me, and affected my health. I wondered if the other person knew what they had done to me, because in my opinion, they should have.

I understand that we're all different and that what upsets one person may not be something that upsets another, yet in the end, shouldn't we respect each others feelings and boundaries?

So, now what?

I need to forgive myself for allowing this to happen. I don't want to carry the anger within me and forgiveness is the only way to release it.

I need to put the boundaries back in place, although the hurt and damage from them being crossed is already done, yet I know with all my heart that more wonderful things will come out of this experience! Hearts will become stronger, relationships will grow and flourish, and life will go on, perhaps better than before the boundaries were crossed.

It's a life lesson, and as much as I write about it, it's a lesson I needed to remember. The Universe whacked me once again, waking me up to something important: I stopped looking out for my well being and what was good for me, even though I knew that someone else was causing me pain.

Lesson learned.

It's important to have healthy boundaries and to draw the "line in the sand" in your mind to prevent someone from crossing them.

Boundaries let others know that you love and respect yourself enough to set them in the first place.

"The Word 'No' Is A Full Sentence"

"NO" is a full sentence and do you know what that means?

It means that there doesn't need to be an explanation as to WHY you said "no" in the first place.

I've always had trouble telling someone "no," as I'm sure you have as well, whether it's to our children, friends, significant other, or even someone we work with, yet I know there are times I need to say it, and it's usually because it doesn't serve my Highest Good. I could be tired, not feeling well or have too much on my plate at that moment. It could simply mean that I need that down time to just "be" or just don't feel like doing what someone had asked me to do.

It's at those moments that I've always felt compelled to give a full explanation as to WHY I say no, yet over the years I've learned that I don't need to do that. The person on the receiving end of my "no" should respect me enough to accept it.

"NO."

End of story.

Yet, not everyone will accept it.

They are the ones that will keep at you until you give them what they want: a "yes." It's their way of controlling you because of their own insecurities over controlling themselves. It's their way of feeding their own ego by knowing they were able to get what they wanted from you and their way of making you feel "out of control."

Remember this: **"what you allow will continue."**

It's okay to think of yourself first and do what's best for YOU and if that means saying "no" when you need to, then it's a good thing. It's the moments that you find yourself saying "yes" when you mean "no" that can affect those around you, because when you give in to someone you feel frustrated with yourself, and sometimes even defeated that they won. You feel submissive to another. You feel as though they are the puppet master and you are their puppet.

All true statements of how you feel but you don't have to play into the hands of another by "giving in" to them.

Don't let anyone take your power from you or your free will to say "no."

The people who love you will accept a "no," but more importantly, the people who RESPECT you will.

What about the people who don't?

Let them go.

You control your life, make your own boundaries with people and have the choice to "enable their behavior or disable their control."

The choice is always yours.

Think about it.

Remember that **"NO"** is a full sentence.

"The Tornado Of Drama"

The drama that other people can cause is like a tornado sucking in all that's in its' path. No one has control over being caught up in the vortex of it, yet a tornado is a force of destruction created by nature.

Drama is a force of destruction created by another human being.

No one can control the forces of nature, but you can control the forces of drama.

Don't allow yourself to be sucked into the path of human destruction and don't allow yourself to be swept up into the vortex of the drama.

A tornado will eventually lose its' power and end.

Drama will only lose its power if you don't engage with it, feed it and fuel it.

You can't control the behavior of others and you can't always stop the person causing the storm, but you can make the choice to seek shelter from it until it goes away.

Eventually, when the storm of drama isn't being fed it will lose its strength and dissipate, the same way a tornado does.

What's left after the storm of drama loses its strength?

"The truth."

"The Messenger"

"Don't shoot the messenger."

I've never liked that saying because I don't believe that there should be a messenger, and most times when there is it's because of a negative person and situation. It's the "messenger of drama."

If you have something to say to someone then say it to their face. Why involve a third party to continue your drama and feed into your lies? If you truly believe your message, then make it your truth, stand in it, and deliver it directly to the person it's intended for. Don't be a coward and use someone else to do your dirty work.

I'm a believer that if you have something to say to me, good or bad, then say it to me, not to anyone who's willing to listen and please do not send a "third party messenger" to say it. I believe that if you can't say it to me, it's because there's no truth to what you're saying in the first place.

I'm sure we've all had a "messenger" come knocking at our door at least once in our lifetime and from my experience, the messenger is simply a pawn in someone else's game of drama.

Stay out of the tornado of drama, don't answer the door to the messenger, and if the true message is given from the source then take it from where it comes from: someone's insecurity, judgement and jealousy.

What would we gain if we stood in our truth and didn't play into the game of "messengers and drama?"

"Peace."

"Is There A Bullseye On My Forehead?"

I've been the target of other people's bad days more times than I can count. I've been talked down to, had hurtful words thrown at me, been reminded of how unimportant I am, and have been enlightened to the fact that I am of no value to them at all. In fact, I've been checking the mirror just to see if there's a bullseye on my forehead!

I've been judged by someone who never took the time to get to know me, yet believes the gossip they heard about me from someone I have no contact with. They've ignored me, turned their back to me to shut me out of a group conversation and rolled their eyes when I'd given them a hug to say "hello" and "good-bye."

I know in my heart that when people are mean and cruel it's their problem, not mine. It's their insecurities and jealousy. They may think that they have no control over their own life, or they lack self-esteem and self-love. The point is, even knowing these things, it still hurts.

Words hurt and once they've been said out loud, they'll hang in the air forever. You can't take back hurtful things you do, you can't take back treating someone badly and you can't take back disrespecting someone. You can apologize and do what it takes to make up for it but once you do it, the damage is done. You've hurt another human being that most likely didn't deserve it and even if they did, no one has the right to treat another human that way.

I won't stoop down to the level of that type of person, play their game, or treat them as badly as they treated me. I'll be the "bigger person," as my mother used to say, but being the "bigger person" doesn't mean I'll put up with that type of behavior from them again and it doesn't mean I'll continue to be around them. I'll forgive them so that I don't stay angry and upset, but I won't forget what they did and who they proved themselves to be.

So, what do I do to get past those hurt feelings? It depends on who the person was and how much energy I want to waste on them. It's usually not much, but if I'm tired or not feeling well then I'll most likely fill a martini glass with tears and take my hurting heart and go to bed.

The next day I'll wake up and see things more clearly. I remind myself that there are people that project their insecurities and low self-esteem onto others. They don't like seeing the good in others because they can't see the good in themselves. They don't understand how someone can be so positive while going through difficult times and they can't. In other words, I'm reminding myself that I don't deserve to be treated that way and neither do you.

So, what do you do now? Here's my thoughts.

Smile as often as you can and share that smile with others.

Treat others the way you want to be treated and if you can't be kind, please be quiet.

Speak positive words that can make a difference in your life and in the life of another.

Always choose your words carefully and most importantly, "always stay humble and kind."

The world desperately needs that.

"It's Only Projection"

There are some cruel people in this world. They are the ones that judge you, point the finger at you, tell you what's wrong with you and are verbally abusive. It doesn't matter if it's someone you know or a stranger. It's wrong.

It happens all too often without warning and without reason, although there is always a reason that people are cruel. They project their own fears and insecurities onto you, and it's wrong, hurtful, and abusive.

My son was the target of a stranger in a convenience store yelling obscenities at him and saying some downright disgusting comments to him. As a mother, it infuriated me and I wish I had been there when it happened. On the other hand, had it not been my child, I still would have been infuriated because no one has the right to speak to another human being that way.

I've been on the other end of verbal abuse more times than I can count, yet there's one thing I've learned and I want to share with you: those people are projecting their fears and insecurities onto someone else.

They see in someone else what they can't see in themselves and want desperately to see or be.

They see a strength in someone else that they wish they had, but don't because they don't know how to be strong.

They see an open minded person living a happy life, being who they are, and wish they could be that person, but they can't because they're afraid to be their authentic self or don't know who they are.

They're afraid to be judged, harassed or abused by someone, even though they are the ones doing this to others.

Those cruel people have low self-esteem, fear, and insecurities beyond belief.

They don't know how to be any other way than cruel, and more often than not, they don't want to try to be any other way. They make the choice to be judgmental and mean, and someone else will suffer because of their ignorance.

I know all of this to be true but I will admit my heart always breaks a bit when someone is nasty and cruel to my loved ones or me.

I have to remember that it's not really me that they're actually judging. They are judging themselves and taking it out on me.

Be kind, my friends, for you never know what the journey of another human being is like.

Ignore those cruel people and know they are the ones with the problems, not you.

Fear, insecurity, jealousy and low self-esteem are negative emotions that breed negative people.

Don't be one of them.

Be you.

Be the best you that you can be.

"Projection Rejection"

"Projection." It's when someone takes their insecurities and fears and projects them onto you. They truly believe all the negative things that they are saying to you and my hope is that you know where it's all coming from and that it's not coming from you.

The saddest part is not that they're doing it, it's that they believe you to be all of those things that they project onto you.

I've been on the other side of projection and have learned that it's not "me," it's "them." I've taught my children about this as well, that when someone is calling them names or telling them "they're this or that," it's someone else's fear and insecurity speaking. The words still hurt, as does the heart, yet we all have to find the strength to understand where all that negative energy is coming from.

Still, it's hard to have someone tell you negative things about yourself, especially when you know that they're not true. The hardest part is knowing that they mean what they say. I believe that's what hurts the most and I'll say it again: it hurts because the person you thought had cared about you believes the negative things that they are saying to you.

What do we do about this thing called "projection?" You need to learn to take it from where it comes from, someone else. We are in control of our own feelings and emotions, and so are they. We can find the resources to understand those feelings and move on from them, and so can they. We know deep down inside that they are projecting their negative emotions onto us, and so do they. It still hurts and as I've been taught throughout the years, you need to learn to block it. You need to understand that it's not you, it's them. You need to see the truth of who they are and deal with the pain in knowing that those terrible things they are telling you about yourself are the things they believe about you and you know they're not true.

We know who we are and aren't. We know our good points and our not so good points. We know that the last thing we need is someone telling us that we're worthless, or that everything is our fault, or that we're not deserving of respect and compassion.

The one real truth I know to share with you is that it's important to set up healthy boundaries for yourself, love yourself enough to keep someone from crossing them and if they continually cross them, ask yourself why you allowed it.

Projection is a negative action and the person who uses that is doing so because they're not in control of their own lives or emotions and simply want others to feel the same. After all, misery loves company!

Be mindful of the people who you surround yourself with. The right people will lift you up, support you, and will want everything FOR you. The wrong people will bring you down, not support you, and will want everything FROM you.

There will always be people that project their low self-esteem, jealousy and insecurities onto others.

Please remember that it's them, not you.

So, what about those "projection" people?

They're not your people.

"No Response Is A Powerful Response"

I love conversation and communication, as most who know me would tell you, yet sometimes situations arise in which communication is NOT key and it's not key because of the person provoking the situation. I believe that we are in control of our lives, of how we feel, react or respond, and who we allow in our circle. We try and live our best life by setting healthy boundaries, yet there are those who don't respect the boundaries we make. They cross the line and do as they please. They gossip, they spread lies and they try and make your life miserable. It's "disrespect" at its' finest.

I used to believe that communication with someone crossing the line was the answer and the right thing to do, yet there are those that want you to do that because it fuels their drama and truth be told, you're giving them what they want: your attention.

I made a choice to stop giving my attention to someone who doesn't deserve it. It's a waste of my precious time and filled with negative energy, and in the end, most times there is no resolution.

I've learned that the best thing for me is NOT to give the situation and the person my precious time and energy. Life is too short to be wasted on the drama that another person causes. It's their insecurities and jealousy that cause them to behave in that way.

I honestly believe that there are times that "no response is a powerful response."

I'll communicate with the people important to me, but I will not engage with someone who isn't.

I can't control the drama that someone else is trying to cause in my life, but I can control how I respond.

My response is "no response."

"Who Really Cares?"

It can be hurtful when the people you care about show you their true colors. You believe that you know someone until a moment comes when they are the complete opposite of who you believed them to be.

I know that feeling all too well but I believe with all my heart that these situations happen to open our eyes to the people we surround ourselves with. It's as if it's a sign that we should be more careful of who we allow in our bubble.

I have to ask myself: "Do they really care about me or do they care about what I have to offer them?" It's a good question and it's the truth in the answer that can either be painful or a confirmation that they do care.

I can't tell you how often I'm checking in with the ones I love and care about to see how their day is going or how they're feeling. I know that just a simple message can mean a lot to them because it's confirmation that I do care about them and want them to know that I'm thinking of them.

On the other hand, I'd like to have the confirmation that they feel the same way about me, but I don't always get that. I can't tell you how often I'm in a conversation with someone who needs me to listen to them but loses sight that I might need to talk as well. I find that I'm the one always reaching out to someone with no response back.

I get tired of that. I'm tired of being forgotten, of not meaning as much to someone as they mean to me and quite frankly, tired of being taken for granted.

What do you do when you start seeing a side of someone that you hadn't seen before?

What do you do when you realize that someone doesn't care as much about you as you do for them?

What do you do when the truth of who they really are appears in front of you?

You re-evaluate the people that you surround yourself with.

This can be a painful process, but an important one because, often times, it's your family, close friends or significant other that you've seen the true colors of.

Your time is valuable and chasing after someone who doesn't care about you is a waste of it.

I don't want to waste my time on the wrong people.

I want to spend my time with the right people.

Surround yourself with people who care about you as much as you care about them. If you're continually chasing the wrong people, you're losing sight of the right people.

Who really cares?

The right people do.

"There Are Times"

Everyone deserves to be treated with kindness and it can come in different forms at different times.

There are times that someone needs your compassion.

There are times that someone needs your time to listen and understand.

There are times that someone needs you to be empathetic towards them.

There are times that someone needs you to be mindful of their feelings.

There are times that someone needs you to say you're sorry and mean it.

There are times that someone needs your actions to make your words true.

There are times that someone needs you to treat them as well as they treat you.

There are times that someone needs you to tell them how much you appreciate them.

There are times that someone needs you to tell them that you love them.

There are times that someone needs you to let them know you're thinking of them.

There are times that someone needs you to let them know that they are important.

There are times that someone needs you to be as kind to them as they are to you.

There are times that someone needs you to give them your support.

And there are times that someone needs to be able to tell you what they need.

Do you know when those times are?

ALL THE TIME!

Please be kind.

"The Art of Forgiveness"

"Everything is forgivable, but not everything is repairable."

I wrote this quote many years ago when I was going through a difficult time of having my heart and soul broken on a daily basis. It was at a time when I listened to someone telling me all that was wrong with me and living through the pain of verbal and emotional abuse.

I had to forgive the person who treated me that way as well as all the people in my life who had treated me badly.

Some would ask me: "why would you forgive someone who hurt you?"

The answer is simple but the process of forgiving someone isn't always easy. I forgive to let go of my anger, but I don't forgive to forget what they did.

Forgiveness isn't about telling the person who hurt you that you forgive them, it's about releasing the anger from within you. You don't forgive them for THEM, you forgive them for YOU!

I believe that everything is forgivable but not always repairable. The people you hurt may forgive you, but they will never forget what you said or did to cause them pain. People will always remember how you made them feel.

Be a person who is mindful and respectful of the feelings of others, especially those you love and care about.

Keep in mind that if you hurt them, they can forgive you but the damage you caused may not be repairable.

Think before you speak and act. Your words are as important as the actions you need to make them the truth.

Be kind.

Be careful with the heart of another.

CHAPTER FOUR

"A Breath About Down Days"

"Crazy Week"

I have "crazy weeks" every so often and I want to share a particular one with you. It was one of ups and downs, sadness and happiness, tears and laughter. It was a week of wondering why all of it was happening and of trying to figure out what the final outcome would be. It was a week of trying to see the life lessons in all that had happened and what changes I was supposed to make in my life because of them.

Then one day something happened to me. I guess you could say I had hit my "rock bottom."

I have a glass topped high table and chairs on my cement patio. I was sitting in the chair when suddenly it broke straight out from under me and I fell down onto the cement patio. Ouch! Needless to say, I was in a lot of pain the next day, walking and sitting much more carefully than usual. I was extremely lucky that I wasn't hurt more than I had been and that I hadn't fallen back onto my head.

I began to think that maybe this random accident was a sign that no matter how far you fall, you have a choice to stay down or get back up.

I got back up.

Life can be amazing, it can be awful, and it can be ordinary, yet what's important is what we do to get through those times.

The crazy week that we all have at times eventually ends and we move forward into another new week and another new day.

"Breathe in the amazing, hold on through the awful, relax and exhale during the ordinary."

Always remember that even though you fall sometimes, you can always get back up.

"HINDSIGHT"

**"Hindsight is the ability to see in the present
what we were unable to see in the past."**

How many times have you found yourself asking these questions: "Why didn't I know better or see the red flags and the writing on the wall?" We think to ourselves: "I wish I had known then what I know now."

I've said it many times throughout my life and I understand it much differently now. Hindsight is when we see something now that we hadn't seen before, but give yourself a break on this one. The reason you see it now is because you grew as a person and learned some life lessons about the people in your life and yourself. You may not have been ready to see it then and are meant to see it now.

Don't beat yourself up or blame yourself because you didn't see something you should have until now. Maybe you weren't meant to see the truth until a certain point in your life. Maybe you were in a certain situation in which you needed to learn and grow. Maybe you were unable to see the truth because you weren't sure of your own truth.

The day will come when you will understand why it all happened and why you didn't see it sooner.

It will be a good day knowing you grew as a person and are moving even further towards the life you want and deserve.

Hindsight.

It's just another way that we learn important life lessons along the journey.

"A Sadness In Your Heart"

Did you ever have a sadness in your heart and for the life of you can't figure out why? Tears well up in your eyes and you just want to let them spill out, and eventually they will flow. It's that feeling of not knowing what's wrong, trying to figure out why you feel sad, and just trying to get through the day of feeling that way.

I have those kind of days every now and again. Those sad days aren't always happening because I'm not happy, it just means that something in my life is out of balance and I need to think about what that is.

So many things can cause us to feel that sadness in our heart: the change in seasons, being cooped up in the house for too long, not getting enough fresh air and sunshine, or not feeling well. We can also feel that sadness if our life isn't going exactly as we had planned and we don't know how to change the direction. It can also happen if we feel invisible or taken for granted in our relationship or friendships. There are many different things that can cause this feeling. Sometimes it's many things, sometimes it's one thing and sometimes it's nothing.

Sometimes it's just our soul trying to tell us that we need to find our balance again and that perhaps in the throws of everyday life we "lost" ourselves again.

It's alright to feel the sadness as long as you don't stay in that place for too long.

After all, it's those "sad" moments that come to teach us something about ourselves and our life. It's those times that are bringing us a life lesson and come to remind us to love ourselves the way we love everyone else in our life.

It's these moments that bring to our attention the fact that we're losing ourselves, that we're not making ourselves as important as we make others feel, or that we're not paying attention to all the signs around us.

Feel the sad moment and remember that this too shall pass. After all, "everything happens as it should, when it should, and how it should."

Take this sad moment as time for yourself to rest, think, and get back to making yourself a priority because you are important. We all are.

Be grateful for the occasional sad moments because without them we'd never truly know what happiness is.

It's just another life lesson in the making.

Go find your balance and go find yourself.

> **"It's the times we feel most sad and lost that turn out to be the times that we're actually finding ourselves."**

"When A Sadness Creeps In"

Every now and again a sadness can creep into you soul, your life, or your day. It's a sadness so deep that it feels as though there's no way out. It's feeling as if a cement brick is lying on your chest and you can't breathe. It's a feeling of being so low that you can't see the light above you.

It's been my experience that those feelings happen when a life lesson we learned long ago comes creeping back in to remind us of what we forgot. It's a feeling of deja vu, that we've been there, done this, and lived through this before. We're left with emotions that we thought were healed years ago.

Then, one day we realize that they're back.

Don't you just hate when you find yourself in a situation in the present that you had fought so hard to heal from in the past? I know I do.

I go through those experiences every so often when I'm not paying enough attention to the behaviors of those around me.

I'll find myself feeling as if I'm back to square one, beating myself up for allowing someone to treat me badly again. I feel angry at myself for ignoring the red flags and missing the signs.

I don't like it, not one bit.

I find myself saying: "Shame on me for allowing someone to treat me in a way less than I deserve, for letting them blame me for their mistakes and for allowing them to make me feel worthless."

Shame on me for allowing it to happen.

Shame on them for believing that they have the right to treat someone badly.

Forgive the abuser so you can let go of the anger.

Forgive yourself for allowing them to treat you badly.

Forgiveness lets the healing begin and enables you to get back to moving forward with your life.

It was just another life lesson that you had forgotten.

Now you've been reminded.

Take that lesson, remember it and go out and live your best life.

"It's Okay To Be Quiet"

Did you ever feel so overwhelmed or stressed that you just can't take the "noise" swirling around you? I know I have and when that happens I get quiet. I literally stop talking, stay off the phone, turn off the music and embrace being "quiet."

Allowing yourself to be quiet can be a good thing for your physical and mental well-being. It's in those moments of quiet that we can be still and collect our thoughts. We can slow down our racing heart rate and relax our body. We can hear the beautiful sounds of nature around us and we can begin to soothe our soul.

I think most of us feel guilty when we get quiet, but we shouldn't. Knowing how you feel and what to do to feel better is a huge part of self-care. It's important to know yourself and what you need to do to live your best life. It's important to find some quiet time during the day so that you are able to hear your intuition speak to you.

It's perfectly okay to want to turn off the world when you're having a down day.

Turn off your cell phone if you don't feel like talking.

Log out of your computer if you don't feel like looking at your emails or social media.

Shut off the television if you don't feel like watching it.

It's okay to be quiet.

There are times when that is exactly what you need to do.

"Dark Clouds"

Do you believe that something wonderful can be born out of something "not so wonderful?"

I do and I bet I can make you a believer, too!

I had a "not so good" comment from someone on my social media page, to which I responded back. It's what transpired from that which became a lesson for all of the people responding to the comment and to myself as well.

I learned that we can't assume that everyone always knows what we're talking about and that is called "miscommunication." I can't tell you how important and absolutely necessary "communication" between one another really is. It's the difference between taking something the wrong way and understanding what someone is really saying.

One of my followers and I mended fences through my page and found out that we had much in common. We both apologized to one another for our miscommunication. It brought so much joy to my heart to be part of a string of comments that had the most beautiful outcome, and it brought even more joy to read the comments from others who had been following it all.

It's true confirmation that "sometimes the most beautiful things come out of the darkest of clouds."

We have to keep our minds and our hearts open to see it.

It was that one post that was proof that we can make a difference in another life and in the world and that we can absolutely do it together.

Be kind.

Be you.

Be open to what lies behind the darkness, because behind the darkness lies the light.

"Did You Ever?"

Did you ever have a day when you wonder what you did wrong?

Did you ever have a day when you wonder why someone seems so distant?

Did you ever have a day when you wonder if you're really loved?

Did you ever have a day when you wonder if the people in your life are real or just what they want you to see?

I have.

I can feel those emotions to my toes.

I feel like everything is my fault.

I feel like it's all "me."

I feel like I'm the one with the problem.

I feel like I AM the problem.

Then I have to stop myself and think.

I have to close my eyes, take the deepest breath I can and clear my mind of all the junk and negative thoughts that have taken up residence in it. I have to be still. I have to be silent. I have to bring myself back to "me."

It's during that moment of stillness that I can hear the answer, or maybe it's the question, but whatever it is, I need to hear it: "Do you really think everything is your fault? It's not. It's them, not you."

I sometimes find that it's hard to believe that it's NOT me. I've lived a lifetime of always believing that everything was MY fault, that I caused the pain in others, that I was the problem and that I was never good enough.

I know differently now.

Each of us has our own journey to experience and our own emotions to feel. NO ONE PERSON is at fault for how someone else feels. We all have feelings and it's our right to feel how we feel.

I've learned throughout the years that I'm not responsible for the feelings of others. I'm living as the best person I can possibly be, and maybe, just maybe, my best isn't always good enough for some people.

And that's okay.

It means that they're "not my people."

Some people need more than I can give because they can't give that to themselves.

I sit here with this one thought: "If you're feeling upset or angry and just want to be left alone, please let me know that it's not because of me."

Tell me that it's you, not me.

I can handle that.

I can handle your wanting to be left alone if I know that I didn't cause it, and no one should assume that the other person knows that.

No one's feelings are wrong but taking it out on another person is.

Let the people you care about know that it's not them, it's you.

That's one step closer to an understanding between two human beings.

"Keeping Your Mouth Shut"

There are moments that we find ourselves "keeping our mouth shut." We hold in the emotions we're feeling and the words we want to speak out loud are locked inside of us. We suffer alone rather than share our pain with someone else.

Do you know why we do that? Fear.

It's the fear of the outcome of being vulnerable.

It's the fear of someone getting angry at us for feeling the way we do or saying what we need to say.

It's the fear of finding out that no one really wants to share our pain with us because the bottom line is that they don't really care. I think that we're all afraid to find out the truth of someone that we thought cared about us.

I understand that "fear" because I used to be the girl that kept her mouth shut, held in her emotions and words, and made the choice to suffer in silence.

There have been more times than I can count in which I have shared my intimate thoughts with someone, only to find out that my being vulnerable to them was not in my best interest. They used that vulnerability to be unkind, mean or cruel. It was a heartbreaking lesson to learn and one I continue to learn now and again, but it was a good lesson to learn.

It taught me to trust others when they've earned it.

It taught me that anyone who takes advantage of my vulnerability is not the person I want in my life.

It taught me to believe that the actions of others speaks louder than their words, and while their words may sound as if they care about you, their actions need to back them up to make them true.

I'm not the girl who keeps her mouth shut anymore and I've come to realize how we DO become that girl or that guy: we surround ourselves with the wrong people.

That's how I learned to know who the right and the wrong people were to have in "bubble."

I learned that the right people accept us for who we are and the wrong people expect us to be who they want.

The right people want everything FOR you and the wrong people want everything FROM you.

Next time you find yourself keeping your mouth shut, holding in your feelings and emotions, or suffering in silence, take a good look at the people around you.

Are they accepting you for who you are or are they expecting you to be who they want?

Do they take advantage of your vulnerability?

Do their actions make their words true?

Only you know the answer and only you can decide who you allow in your bubble.

Choose what's best for you.

CHAPTER FIVE

"A Breath About Being Positive"

"Get Excited"

"Find something to get excited about."

You don't have to wait for something big to happen in your life to get excited. You have the power to make your life exciting, from the smallest of things to the biggest, and you can always find something to get excited about.

Get excited about that first cup of coffee in the morning while sitting in your favorite spot.

Get excited about checking another task off of your "to do" list.

Get excited about taking a day off for yourself with no real plans in place.

Get excited about driving in your car, taking a long walk, or working out at the gym.

Get excited about your favorite song playing on the radio.

Get excited about someone smiling at you.

Get excited about having a great conversation with someone.

Get excited about laughing out loud.

Get excited about love.

Get excited about making a difference in someone's life.

Get excited about your life.

Don't save feeling "excited" for a big moment to happen when there are so many small moments to be excited about.

Live your life out loud, to the fullest and with gratitude!

Remember, you can always find something to get excited about.

You can start today!

"Do Life Happy"

Happiness is one of the best emotions in the world and I love when I have a day or more of feeling as if I'm on Cloud Nine. I have to say, it's that type of happiness that can make me tired but I know I'll also be sleeping better. I'll find myself dancing in the kitchen while I'm cooking or cleaning, or I'll be singing out loud to the song on the radio while I'm driving. I'll be smiling from ear to ear and laughing like never before. It's so much more than happiness, I'm feeling "joy," and I'm "doing life happy!"

I made a decision to stop "trying" to let things go. I've had enough of wasting my precious energy on "trying" to let things go. It's time to stay out of situations that aren't my problem or concern so that there's nothing to let go. There have been moments in which I've wanted to get involved to help, but now I remind myself that it's not my problem, it's someone else's and truth be told, if I fix their problem they'll never learn the lesson that they were supposed to.

I'll always be there for anyone who needs me, whether it's my advice, a shoulder to cry on or simply my ear to listen, yet I'm I'm beginning to understand more and more that I can't allow the problems of someone else to become mine.

We all have life lessons to learn, be it your children, family, friends or significant other, and when we interfere with their free will to handle the situation in the way that they want, we've taken away their right to learn from it. We've allowed the negativity and toxicity of their situation to affect us as well, and that won't serve anyone well.

Life would be so much easier if someone else could fix our problems, heal our hearts, and tell us what we need to do to live a happy life, yet that's not how life works, nor should it. We need to learn how to fix our own problems, heal our own hearts, and learn to know what it is we need to do (or not do) to be happy. We need to learn our life lessons so that we can live the best and happiest life possible.

We all have a choice to be happy or not, face our demons and problems or not, and to learn from them or not. I'm a person who decided to make those choices for my Highest Good. I decided that I wanted to live a happy life and have learned how to do so. I decided to face those demons along the journey of my life, deal with them and heal from them. I decided that all things happen for a reason and that I would take those lessons and learn from them. The bottom line is this: we all need to learn to love ourselves and believe that we deserve all good things.

I'm here for anyone who needs me. If you need to use my shoulder to cry on, you got it. If you need an ear to tell your problems to, I'm listening. If you need to know how I handled my difficult situations in life and how I got through them, I'll tell you and if you just need to know you're not alone, I'll tell you that you're not because I'll be there for you.

I'm still the same person I've always been and still working on growing into the best sense of self I can possibly be, but in order to do that I've had to learn what and who is best for me.

There will be no more "trying" to let things go, unless those things belong to me.

"Look In The Mirror"

Please be kind. Be kind to everyone. The world is in desperate need of it.

Don't be the person who puts your back to someone to exclude them from being part of the group.

Don't be the person who rolls your eyes when someone takes the time to hug you.

Don't be the person who treats someone badly because of someone else's opinion and judgement of them.

Be the person that always leaves a space open for someone to be part of the group.

Be the person who hugs someone back with eyes filled with gratitude that they thought enough of you to hug you in the first place.

Be the person who treats everyone kindly, whether you like them or not.

I don't know of anyone who wants to be treated badly or disrespected. It's hurtful.

My solution for getting past their behavior is to say to yourself: "Who cares?"

You may feel blindsided or hurt by their behavior, but in the end, you're the better and bigger person who didn't stoop to their level. They should care more about what YOU think of their behavior, yet they won't.

The "don't be the person" is small minded, even weak minded. I'll go as far to say that they don't have a mind of their own. They base their opinions on the opinions of others, gossip, lies, insecurity and jealousy. They enjoy belittling others, making them feel small and unimportant when the truth of the matter is, they themselves feel small and unimportant.

I have no time for anyone, friend or family, that treat me badly or put me down. I have no tolerance for someone turning their back towards me in a group to let me know they don't want to include me. I have no respect for the people that are part of that group to allow that bad behavior.

What I do have are choices. I have a choice to distance myself from the situation, even leave it completely. I have a choice to continually put myself in this type of situation or respect myself never to do it again. I have a choice to never see that person, or people, again.

They're not important. They've just shown you who they are. They don't care about you, even though you believed that they did.

There are so many other people that are more important. They are the people who always have your back, who look into your eyes and who can't wait to be with you.

Those are the people who lift you up, not knock you down.

Those are the people who are kind to you, respect you for who you are, and who don't judge you based on the opinions of others.

Those are YOUR people. Don't settle for less than that.

Take a look in the mirror. Which person are you?

"What You Give Makes You Rich"

"What makes a person rich isn't how much they have, but how much they give."

It's that "kindness" thing again. We all have the ability to be kind to one another and to help someone in need. It doesn't matter if you don't have the money to give, what matters is what you can give from your heart.

The heart can give love, support, compassion, understanding, consideration, respect and the willingness to be there for someone who needs a shoulder to cry on or a listening ear. None of that costs a thing. Kindness is FREE!

Let's do this together. Let's spread kindness throughout this world.

If someone needs your help, then help them in whatever way you can.

If someone feels sad or hurt, then love them through the pain.

If someone is feeling sick, then ask them what you can do to help them feel better.

Think about the people in your life that are kind to you, always there for you, that love you through difficult times, take care of you, and that help you when you need help.

Doesn't that make you feel loved? Doesn't that make you feel safe to know there's someone there for you? Doesn't that make you feel good to know that someone is kind to you?

I'm sure you do.

The question is this: Are you doing the same for those people or anyone else that may need your kindness? Are you helping someone you know that needs your help? Are you there for the people who are there for you?

Be grateful for the people who are kind to you. Be sure to share that kindness back to them so that they can be grateful for you.

Let's spread kindness today and everyday, to the people you know and the ones that you don't.

Kindness can change the life of another human being and it can change the world.

If we stick together and spread kindness to everyone, it WILL change the life of another human being and it WILL change the world.

"ENTHUSIASM"

"When you are enthusiastic about what you do, you feel this positive energy. It's very simple." ~Paul Coehlo~

That is such a true statement and it's not just about your life purpose or your job. It's about everything. It's about being enthusiastic, happy, and joyful about everything you do.

Smile when you pour that first cup of coffee or tea in the morning.

Be happy when you're driving to work or running errands.

Feel joyful when you're cooking a meal for your family or friends.

You see, when you do everything, from the big things to the small with enthusiasm, you attract positive energy and that energy spills onto those around you.

It's hard to imagine doing mundane tasks with tons of enthusiasm, yet I know for sure that if you can change your mindset, you can find joy even in those tasks.

Find joy in everything that you do.

Laugh every chance you can.

Smile from ear to ear.

Be enthusiastic about your life.

It's amazing how wonderful life can be when you change your mindset and find enthusiasm for your life.

"Under The Tree, Just Me"

—◦◦❦◦◦—

"Sit and wonder under the tree, just me. Breathe and dream you will know everything under the tree."

I have a beautiful tree in my backyard that I love to sit beneath. I call it my "magic" tree. It's right outside of my back door and the moment you step outside, you're under it. It's the place where I have my morning coffee and where I sit when I need a bit of peace and serenity during the day.

It's a hermosa tree, but I started calling it the magic tree almost seven years ago. Let me tell you why.

This tree springs back to life when winter is done and over with, and each year it seems to grow another six feet out from the house. It shields us from the rain and is a shady spot when the sun is shining bright. Each year my family and I look forward to seeing just how much it has grown throughout the winter months and it never disappoints us. It's as if we have a natural canopy enveloping our backyard.

It possesses a type of magic I've never felt before. It's the place I go to sit and think, have my morning coffee or a glass of wine at night. The answers to my questions always come to me more easily under the tree. Any problems I have seem to be solved while looking up at it and it's given me more ideas for writing than I could have ever asked for.

The leaves close up as the sun goes down and open back up when the sun rises in the morning. It drops subtle drops of water throughout the day as if it were crying. It blooms fluffy pink flowers on the tops which drop at our feet when we're under it. It's as if the tree has a mind of its own.

It's as if it knows what we need: peace.

My "happy place" living at the Shore is on the water, but my "magic tree" is my "happy place" at home.

I'm grateful every morning I wake up to be able to sit under my "magic tree."

Everyone needs a "happy place" of their own. It's that place where you find peace and serenity.

It's that place that relaxes your body and soothes your soul.

It's that place where you can go to just "be."

Where is your "happy place?"

"The View From My Desk"

My desk sits right at the front window of my home. It's a great view of the neighborhood, of the changing shadows and light, and of the trees and the birds. It doesn't matter what time of day it is, the view is peaceful and calm, and something that I'm truly thankful for.

One of the perks of this view is that I have this one particular bird who has become bold enough to fly right up to my front window and hover there for a few minutes. This sweet little bird is one of my favorites: it's a hummingbird!

I'm fascinated with these creatures, from the way they fly to the way they hover for a bit of time. This year there seems to be more of them frequenting the feeder that hangs from my magic tree in the backyard, but one in particular has become much braver. He will fly right up to my front window and look at me as if to say: "Hi, how's it going? What are you writing today?"

I'm grateful to have a desk with this view, for the sights and sounds that I can see and hear from it, and that each time I look up from my computer and look out the window there is always something new to see.

I'm grateful for this little hummingbird that makes my day each time he comes to visit me at the front window.

Life is full of some amazing surprises and sometimes they're right outside of your front window.

Keep your eyes open!

"Here Comes The Sun"

It's been days of heavy rain, steady winds, and dark skies here at the Shore. In other words, the weather has been awful and everyone I know in this area has been feeling the same way: tired and worn out.

Yet this morning, much to my surprise, I woke up to a room flooded in sunlight! It's true, the sun has come out again at the Shore and I couldn't be happier. I'm sure everyone else who lives here feels the same.

As I grabbed my coffee and headed outside to sit under blue skies and bright sunlight, all I could hear in my head was a few lines from a Bob Marley song: "Don't worry, 'bout a thing, cause every little thing's gonna be alright."

It's so true. Every time that I'd spoken with someone on the phone or scrolled down social media during the days that the sun had stayed hidden, I could see that everyone was going through something. It was as though everyone was feeling down and life's little problems were manifesting into big ones.

Today, with the sun shining bright, I bet that all those big problems will lessen and will once again become "little problems" that you are better able to handle. They may turn out to have not been a problem at all.

Never underestimate the power of the sun. It can brighten the darkest of moods and give you a burst of energy. It's a natural source of Vitamin D and it increases serotonin levels in your brain which elevates your mood and makes your start believing again that "every little thing's gonna be alright."

So, today if you're lucky enough to live in an area in which the sun is shining, get outside and soak up those beautiful rays.

Remember, no matter what's going on in your life right now, you're doing just fine and so am I.

Every little thing really will be alright.

Hold tight, breathe through it and soak up those glorious rays of the sun every chance you get.

"JUST IMAGINE"

My friend, Mark, sent me a picture of his favorite hat. It had the words "Just Imagine" on it.

It started me thinking about what I would "just imagine." Take a moment and let's all "just imagine" a different world, a different way to live, a different perspective.

Just imagine a world in which:

Everyone was kind to one another.

Everyone treated one another with respect and compassion.

Everyone would choose their words carefully and communicate with each other in a calm and respectful manner.

Everyone cared about each other.

Everyone was honest and truthful and dishonesty never existed.

Everyone supported each other.

Everyone helped those who needed help and expected nothing in return.

Everyone was grateful for the people in their life and didn't take them for granted.

Everyone appreciated each day they were blessed to have.

Everyone stopped projecting their insecurities and fears onto others and realized that their behaviors were emotionally and verbally abusive.

Everyone strived to be a good person and their best sense of self.

Everyone was grateful for another day to live their best life.

Everyone who says "I love you" to someone means it and has the actions to make those words the truth.

Everyone stopped complaining about what they don't have and were grateful for what they do have.

Everyone put the effort in to get along with others."

Imagine what it would be like if everyone wanted to do all of those things together, if everyone wanted to come together to change this world into the beautiful place it's meant to be, and if everyone could learn that kindness matters to those that you know and those that you don't.

Just imagine this type of world.

Just imagine how we could change it TOGETHER.

"Sometimes We Need To Know"

I'm a "need to know" kind of girl. I don't assume how others feel about me but want to KNOW how they feel about me, and I want to feel it to my toes.

I know that loving yourself first is the key to living your best life, but I'll tell you this, knowing that someone loves you is just as important. The right words count but the actions make them truth. It doesn't matter if it's your partner, your family or your friends, sometimes we just "need to know" how they feel.

We "need to know" that what they say is the truth and not a lie, that we can trust them with our heart and feelings, and that if they say one thing they don't do another.

We "need to know" the truth.

We usually need this type of confirmation when we're going through rough times or feeling scared about something.

We need to know because we may feel as if we're being taken for granted, that someone we love lost sight of us, or we feel used by someone who we're always there for but who aren't always there for us.

As for me, the "need to know" isn't in the grand gestures, it's in the small ones, because to me, it's those "small" things that mean so much more than the "big" ones. And here's some of the "small" things that mean the most to me:

~Getting a call, a text or message from someone who just wants me to know they were thinking about me.

~Finding a note near my computer or on my dresser to make me smile (my son does this every so often for me and it means so much!)

~It's handpicked flowers for no special occasion.

~It's someone making your coffee for you or knowing that you like your ice water with lemon.

~ It's someone taking the time to listen to you.

~ It's someone offering a hug because they know that you needed one, not because you asked.

~It's someone respecting you enough to be honest with you even though you may not like what they have to say.

~It's someone telling you that you're loved, important and a priority to them and making sure you know that by their actions.

~It's someone doing something to make you smile or laugh or both.

I love the small gestures.

They're the ones that take thought and simply knowing that someone was thinking of you during their busy day is priceless.

We all have those "need to know" moments and isn't it a beautiful thing when we know?

"Hope"

My closest of friends tell me that they're amazed that I'm such a hopeful person. You can forget about the phrase, "hopeless romantic," I'm a "hopeful romantic!" They're right, though, I am always hopeful.

I don't see the challenge, I see the opportunity it can afford you.

I don't see the risk in taking a leap of faith, I see the chance for something better.

I don't see the heartache in life as life threatening, I see it as life changing.

I don't see anything in life that there isn't "hope" for.

I'm hopeful that people can change if they want to.

I'm hopeful that an ending to something can bring a beautiful beginning.

I'm hopeful that the world can change into a better one.

I'm hopeful that we will always find our strength even when we feel weak.

I'm hopeful that the obstacles we face on our journey are to teach us something about ourselves that will help us live our best life.

You see, I believe that "hope heals." It may not always heal in the way you wish it to, yet it will help to heal you. The Universe is always looking out for us and as I always say, "everything happens as it should, when it should, and how it should."

Don't lose hope in difficult situations. Find the hope and keep the faith.

As Christopher Reeve said, "Once you choose hope, anything's possible."

I believe that with all my heart because I know there's healing in the hope.

"Blinded By The Light"

I wake up each morning with gratitude for being gifted another day to live my best life and to do what it takes to make a positive impact in the life of another and in the world.

I was thinking about the people that I'm blessed to have in my life: my family and my friends.

I was thinking about all the things that bring me joy: my home, my writing, and my life of living at the Jersey Shore.

I was thinking about the smallest of things that bring me peace: my morning coffee, the smell of the salt air, the sounds of the ocean, the sunrises and sunsets.

So often we lose sight of all the beauty that surrounds us because of the "ugly" things that try to blind us.

Keep your eyes open to see the beauty that surrounds you and let your light shine.

After all, "ugly" is always blinded by the light.

"Just Believe"

Isn't it amazing how the Universe works? Do you know that feeling I'm talking about? It's when suddenly everything starts coming together, that all the dreams you have been working towards begin turning into reality, and that suddenly people, situations and opportunities are falling into your lap. It's when everything just seems to be falling into place in your life.

I love when that happens to me and I love when I see it happening to other people. There's no need to question why it's suddenly happening, but accept that it is happening just when it was meant to.

I love that these moments give me so much positive energy, more focus, and an even better understanding of my life. It can definitely make me feel as though my head is spinning, yet I know it's spinning in the right direction.

I love that I'm learning to let go of the things I can't control or change. I'm moving forward with what I can control and can change, and that is ME!

Life is good, actually, life is wonderful. All the things I've wanted are falling into place and things I didn't even know I wanted are coming into my life.

Embrace the journey.

Let the Universe guide you.

Have patience that everything happens as it should, when it should and how it should.

"Just believe, just have faith, everything else will fall into place."

"Hugs"

More often than not, it's the simplest of things that can make a difference in the life of another. We all possess the ability to help someone feel better, let them know they're not alone, and to be there to listen to them vent or cry or just let it all out.

What makes you feel better when you're feeling down, or sad when someone has hurt your feelings, or you're having a bad day?

For me, it's someone who allows me the comfort of being vulnerable, of shedding my tears and bearing my soul about why I'm hurt. It's someone who listens to me without judgement or let's me cry on their shoulder.

It's someone who doesn't tell me to get over it but helps me get through it.

It's someone who doesn't see the situation or person who hurt me, but only sees the person who is hurt, which would be "me."

I'll always try to protect the people that I love and will always be there for them. My heart will feel their pain right along with them, my arms will be open to hold them and I'll always have my shoulder available for them to cry on.

You see, the person who hurts another gains power when you place your attention and anger on them, rather than where it belongs: with the person who is feeling hurt.

When someone hurts another human being it's their own fears and insecurities that they're projecting on one another and believe me, I'm learning to understand where it comes from. Understanding that doesn't mean I have to tolerate it or them, it means I need to wish them love and light and walk away from them.

Don't give your energy and power to the wrong people.

Give your energy, time, love, listening ear, understanding, compassion, respect and your heart to the right people.

One of the best ways I know of to help someone you love get through their feelings of heartache and hurt caused by another is simple: hug them.

Hug them tight with all the love you have for them in your heart.

Hug them for as long as they need your arms wrapped around them.

Hug them because they are important to you.

One day you'll need that same hug given back to you.

"That's What Love Does"

We don't always understand why someone we love and care about is upset or sad, but we can try.

That's what love does.

Love listens, tries to understand, wraps its arms around you to make you feel safe, and allows you to be who you are.

Love doesn't criticize you, it compliments you.

Love doesn't judge you, it embraces your flaws.

Love helps to heal you but doesn't try to hurt you.

True, honest, unconditional love can do some amazing things.

It's time that we share that love with the people we love.

"Shower the people you love with love, show them the way that you feel."
James Taylor

Because that's what love does.

"Be That Person"

Somewhere in the world there's someone who…

Needs to talk. Be the person who gives them their time and listens.

Needs to cry. Be the person who offers the shoulder for them to do it on.

Needs a hug. Be the person who opens their arms to embrace them.

Needs to feel loved. Be the person who gives it freely.

Needs to be understood. Be the person who hears them.

Needs sound advice. Be the person who gives it without judgement.

Needs a friend. Be the person who is a friend.

Needs someone to hold their hand. Be the person who offers them one.

Needs someone to help them. Be the person who offers their help with no expectations of receiving anything in return.

Sometimes someone just needs to know that you're there for them. Be the person who shows them that you are.

Be that person for someone because someday YOU may need them to be that person for you.

"On My Porch"

The ocean brings me comfort, the mountains bring me peace,
And when I can't get to them there's another place of ease.
It's right outside my front door, illuminated by a torch,
This place is in my rocking chair, this place is my front porch.

It's here I sit and ponder, it's here I sit and stare,
It's here I do my writing and here I have no cares.
My mind is still and quiet, my thoughts so close to touch
I think of life, of all my dreams, of those I love so much.

My front porch holds the magic, the key into my soul,
It's here my mind will wander to thoughts of the unknown.
It's here the realization comes, the answers that I need,
It's in the chair on my front porch that I figure out who's "me."

"Intuition"

There's an intuition, an awareness known to few,

A gift to those who're blessed to know, while others have no clue.

It's that space we all possess, deep within our soul,

The answer to the questions, it's our story to be told.

You need only sit in stillness and bathe yourself in light

To see and hear what's clearly been right there within your sight.

Most will fear its' power while others embrace its strength

Intuition is your soul on fire that speaks to you at length.

Listen, always listen, as your heart and soul are one.

Trust in their guidance, trust in their words,
and the answers all will come.

CHAPTER SIX

"A Breath About Life Lessons"

"Fear"

Do you know what's on the other side of fear? Everything you ever wanted.

Do you know what's above fear? Faith.

Do you know what's around fear? Anxiety, stress, worry and negative emotions.

So why, if we know these things to be true, do we allow "fear" into our vocabulary? Why do we allow or invite "fear" into our life? Why do we succumb to fear rather than rise up in faith?

It's because we're human and have moments in our life when we are afraid.

We're afraid to be abandoned, lose a job, or afraid that we may fail at something we try to do. The list goes on of what we're afraid of but I'm here to tell you that nothing positive is born out of fear.

Fear blocks you from moving forward and living the life you want.

Fear prevents you from trying to catch a dream or take a chance on love.

Fear blocks, limits and keeps you stuck.

What do you do when you're afraid of something? Remind yourself that everything happens for a reason and that what you fear is change in your life.

What happens if you do lose your job? You'll have the chance to find a better job.

What happens if a relationship or friendship ends? A beautiful new beginning of another one could be waiting for you.

What happens when you try to catch a dream and it doesn't happen? A dream that you may never have imagined may come true.

I'm as human as you are and there are moments in my life when fear is just knocking at my door. Sometimes I answer it to see what it wants and, more often than not, it's come knocking to remind me of a life lesson or teach me a new one. Sometimes it comes knocking to simply ask you this question: "What are you so afraid of and WHY?"

That's the key: "WHY are we afraid?"

It's because when we're NOT afraid we're accepting that we can't control everything, that we have to trust something bigger than us, and that we have to trust ourselves and our intuition.

Do you know what I do when fear enters my mind?

I sit with it for a bit. I try to figure out what I'm so afraid of and I have to be honest with myself about WHY I'm afraid.

Once I can do that I can let go of the fear and continue on in my life with faith that everything in my life happens as it should, how it should and when it should.

It always does.

Remember that when fear comes knocking on your door.

"Facing Your Fears"

I survived breast cancer. I faced chemo and radiation, surgery for a port, and countless biopsies, mammograms, MRI's with contrast, a lumpectomy and some other difficult procedures. It was a lot, and I made it through. The initial diagnosis was scary, but I faced my fears.

I survived two divorces and the only thing that had scared me about them was making it on my own with my five children, but I faced my fears.

I survived a cycle of abuse, but I faced my fears.

I've faced many fears but the one that was the hardest to face was this: fear of the dentist!

I knew I had to go to the dentist, yet somewhere along the years I became terrified to go, and other than the discomfort and pain which was sometimes involved, I never really understood why I had this tremendous fear of the dentist.

I did and I knew the time had come to face it.

Chemo had wreaked havoc on my teeth and I was embarrassed of how they looked. I began smiling with my mouth closed, which I hated. I knew I had to get my teeth repaired but how?

I had to face my fear and this was my biggest of all!

I reminded myself of all the things I write about, all the beliefs I have of taking care of yourself, being healthy and living your best life. Now I was feeling guilt. I asked myself, "How can you write about all these positive things for others to do when you're afraid to do them yourself? You write about releasing fear and taking a leap of faith, so what about you?"

I pointed the proverbial finger at myself.

So, in order to live my best life and get back the smile I missed, I called the dental office and made my first appointment.

I was terrified but I decided to face my fears.

My fears lessened each time I went to the office. I was greeted by an amazing team of girls at the front desk". The dental hygienists that worked with my dentist would have mindless conversations with me before the dentist came into my room. I knew what they were doing: trying to calm my nerves.

Yet it was my dentist who was the person who helped me face my fears and get past them. She was awesome, to say the least, and I'm forever grateful that she has the patience of a saint when it came to me.

It was months of going to the dentist, each appointment no longer or shorter than two hours. I was in her chair at least once a week to get all the work done that was needed. I thank Dr. Diane for alleviating my fears and helping me face them. She gave me the smile back that I had missed and knew that I deserved to have again.

I still remember the day all the work was done and she held up the mirror for me to look into. I held back tears of joy in seeing the effects of chemo on my teeth gone and now seeing the effects of a wonderful dentist who brought back my smile.

My fears of the dentist no longer exist, and I look forward to going back for my check-up. I look forward to seeing this amazing group of people at this dentist office and am forever grateful to all of them, especially my dentist.

Face your fears. Let others help you get through them if you need to. It's not always easy, but it's always worth it.

As for me, it's all "smiles" here!

"Deal and Feel"

I've gone through my share of what most may say were incredibly painful experiences: divorce, cancer, and abuse, to name a few. When I share these experiences publicly many people ask me how I'm still standing or how in the world did I become so positive after so many negative things happened to me.

My answer is always the same: "It's because I made a choice to get through those experiences and deal with the pain that they had caused and because of that, I'm standing even stronger."

I knew I had to feel all the emotions that came with those "traumas" and deal with them. It was by dealing with them that I was able to begin the healing process.

No one wants to feel hurt, sadness or brokenness, yet we all do at some point in our life. Many people block those emotions. They tuck them away deep inside of themselves and believe that they moved on from them. I can tell you that they didn't. Ignoring what you have to face is lying to yourself and eventually all those emotions that you didn't deal with will catch up with you at some point in your life. They will come to the surface when you're faced with another trauma. They always do.

When they do catch up with you, those around you may experience your pain as well because you haven't dealt with them.

Don't you want to feel happy? Don't you want to find joy in your life? Don't you want to let go of an experience that caused you pain?

I'm sure you do. We all do.

Now is the time to do it. Now is the time to deal with it and heal from it. Take a look at yourself in the mirror and see your truth. Take that experience and all the pain that came with it and deal with it. Feel the pain, the heartache and let the healing waters of your tears flow to release it all. Forgive the experience so that you no longer hold onto the painful emotions and forgive yourself for allowing it to hold you back from the happiness you want and deserve.

You can run from those traumatic experiences, but trust me, you can't hide from them until you deal with them. They will always rear their ugly heads at some point or another because you haven't released them.

Feel, deal and heal.

Take those traumatic experiences and put them to rest.

You'll be glad that you did.

"Run Over By A Bus"

It was around 7 pm one night that I shuffled into the kitchen and asked my kids if they had gotten the license plate number of the bus that had just run over me. They said "no" but they think it was from out of state. It sure was because I've been "out of my normal state of being" since then.

In other words, I got sick, very sick.

The upper respiratory virus that seems to have been plaguing my area had hit me full force with a cough that I thought would blow my heart out of my chest. I coughed so much since that night that I thought there would be nothing left inside of me, but there was. There was the pain in my rib cage from coughing so hard, the tears flowing from my eyes at the frustration of not being able to sleep, and the crankiness from not being able to function as I normally do.

All negative emotions to a negative sickness.

Yet, it was so much more.

It was my body telling me that it had had enough, that I needed to slow down, rest, and more importantly, take care of MYSELF. It was my body telling me that there was way too much inside of it that needed to come out and it came out through my constant coughing for days on end.

I believe that the ailments of any sickness have a spiritual meaning to them. As far as a cough, it means that we're holding in negative emotions, hurt feelings, or things that we need to get out and we get them out through various ways.

My body was relieving itself of hurt, sadness, pain and negative emotions through my cough. It seemed to be the only way out.

Yes, I have a virus, but I also believe that this virus was my saving grace by forcing me to slow down, rest, take care of myself and let go of all that negative junk inside of me.

After more than a week of hot tea with honey and lemon, countless hot toddies, over- the-counter cough remedies which ended with a visit to the doctor for some heavy duty medication, I began to feel better.

I've coughed it all out for almost a week. I still felt weak and didn't feel quite like my old self, but the cough was lessening and instead of fighting it, I let it run its course and allowed it to teach me to learn to let it all out, in whatever way the Universe saw fit.

For me, it was this never ending cough.

Once I gave into it all, allowed it to slow me down, gave it control over my doing nothing but sit in my recliner for days with a heating pad on my chest, it's lessened, and I could feel myself getting better. I sat in that chair and slept in it for almost a week. I began to resent that chair until I realized that it was part of this journey, an instrument in this lesson, and a comfort when I needed one.

I'm grateful for that chair, grateful for the cough, grateful for the experience, and I'm grateful that after what seemed like an eternity, I was back to feeling healthy again.

Life throws us many curve balls in so many ways, yet it's for our own good. We have to believe that it's all another lesson on the journey.

I've learned my lesson with this experience.

I'm keeping an eye out for the next bus that comes my way!

"What Are You Missing?"

It's sad when I see so many people missing out on the greatest moments of their life. What is so important in their life that they're not enjoying it? I had to wonder.

There are times that I can see why it's happening. It happens when we're so consumed with making a living to pay the bills that we forget to have a life. Aren't we supposed to be working to make a living so that we can ENJOY life?

The job can't bring you what's truly important in life: love, family and friends. The job may bring a paycheck which is sometimes spent soon after it's received, yet the life will bring you memories that can never be spent after you get them. Memories last a lifetime but a paycheck lasts as long as it takes to pay those bills.

It's up to each of us to decide which is more important: our job or our life. The job doesn't hold our friends and families, it holds a title and a paycheck. The life holds our friends and families and more than any paycheck can offer, it holds love.

There are people that I love and care about that are losing sight of their life because of their job. It hurts my heart to watch it because the job turns them into someone unrecognizable to me and the people that love them. The job stresses them out so much that all they can do is find a way to decompress when they get home. The job puts so much pressure on them that they take it out on the ones they love rather the ones they don't: their employers.

A job is a job.

A life is a life.

A job is money.

A life is memories.

I can tell you that my career as a writer and all the work that may come with it will NEVER be a priority over my life with my loved ones. Sure, I have deadlines and marketing to do, days filled with more work than I could have imagined, but it's never changed who I am. I won't take a long day of writing out on those I love because in the end, I love my writing but I love the people in my life more. I know that the really important things in life don't last forever and the job will always end sooner than that.

What's your priority?

Do you want to make memories or make money?

You can find the balance. You can set up boundaries with a job and a boss that could care less about you personally by doing what's expected of you and not what's expected because of you.

Loved ones, life and a job won't last forever.

Go out and make a good living, but more importantly, go out and make a good life!

"Character and Reputation"

My friend, Jonathan, and I always say "no judgement, just an observation," and we mean it. We don't judge one another or anyone else, yet we do observe.

I had a discussion with a friend of mine about people passing judgement on me, a judgement which made them look at me differently than they previously had. The truth of the matter was that I was suddenly being treated as an "outsider" when I had believed that I was an "insider" for years. He asked me if someone said something to them that made them treat me this way and I couldn't imagine that anyone would have.

I told him I was blindsided when I walked into a situation where the air was cold and the mood was one of "what's she doing here?" I was stunned and hurt. Backs were turned towards me and there was no conversation, just idle chit chat. I was relieved when we left the situation soon after because the thirty minutes or so that I spent there with them was thirty minutes too long. I was hurt, humiliated and just wanted to get away from it all and I did.

I realized they were judging me on my reputation, not my character. Reputations are born out of lies, opinions, judgement and gossip. Character is born out of the behavior of someone being their authentic self.

Sometimes I think I'm too "simple" minded of a girl because I truly believe the world can be so much better than it is. I believe that everyone has the ability to be kind to others. I believe that no one has the right to be cruel to another. I believe that together we can all make a positive difference in this world.

Yet sadly, my way of thinking isn't always true for some people.

Yes, the world can be so much better, but not everyone chooses to be kind. There are people that feel as though they have the right to be cruel to someone else, and not everyone believes that they can do anything to change the world.

I will always be positive, always continue to try and make a difference in the life of another and in the world, and always believe that there is hope.

I don't judge anyone but I do observe their behavior. I don't listen to gossip and lies because the truth comes from the individual that's being talked about. I don't take someone's reputation as truth, I'll spend time observing their character.

Everything begins with you and you have a choice.

Do you want to believe the reputation built by others or believe the character built solely by the person?

The choice is yours.

"MAKE EACH DAY COUNT"

Every so often life hands us a scary, almost terrifying moment and I had one that I want to share with you.

I was taking my normal drive to the food store and was approaching a red light on a very busy highway. As I stepped on the brakes to stop, the pedal went straight down to the floor. Thank God I wasn't going too fast or that someone was in front of me because the car slowed enough for me to steer it to the side and let the curb stop me.

I've never had something like this happen to me before and when it did happen I thought it was something as simple the brake fluid. I was wrong.

The brake line had broken.

I am so incredibly grateful it wasn't any worse than it was, because it could have been.

There were definitely some Angels watching over me.

My son, Noah, picked me up. I was shaking and crying when he pulled up and the first words out of his mouth were "Mom, are you okay? Let me hold you."

I cried even more.

I cried because that could have been the last day of my life. I cried because I couldn't imagine someone calling my children to tell them bad news and I cried because I was happy that it wasn't worse.

Yet, as the writer that I am, I've been thinking about what happened and what didn't and the old saying that "no day is promised" kept playing over and over again in my head.

This wasn't a major accident or tragedy, but it could have been.

It wasn't my day to leave this world.

It was my day to be grateful that I didn't.

All I could think about after that incident was how blessed I am. It forced me to re-evaluate some things in my life and to take a long hard look at this life I'm living. It made me think about everything, nothing and all of it.

"No day is promised" yet someone decided that that particular day WAS promised to me and I wasn't going to take that for granted.

I'm grateful that I'm here and able to continue doing what I love: writing, loving the people in my life and trying to make a difference in the world.

I'm always grateful for each day I wake up and have a chance to make a difference, and after that incident, I'm even more grateful and more mindful to never take another day for granted.

Life is a funny thing and I truly believe that everything happens for a reason.

That day happened to me for a reason.

It happened to remind me of what's important and what's not, of who belongs in my life and who doesn't, and how incredibly precious my life is.

Your life is precious as well.

No day is promised.

We never know when our last day is.

Make the most of each day you are gifted to have.

Make a difference in someone's life and in the world.

Make time to be with the ones you love.

Make time each and every day to count your blessings.

"Some Days and Other Days"

There are some days you just want to give in and give up. You're tired of the drama and negativity that other people are bringing into your life, you're exhausted from trying to escape it and them, and you feel helpless because it seems as if you have no control over anything. There are some days you feel sad for every reason and no reason, you cry because you're eyes need to let out the tears, and you feel tired even though you had a good night's sleep.

Those are the "some days."

How about the "other days?"

The days you watch a beautiful sunrise with your morning coffee or spending time with the ones you love as you watch a spectacular sunset.

The days that you see all the beautiful people, places and things that surround you and know that you are blessed.

The days that you check off all the things on your to-do list and feel a sense of accomplishment.

The days that you walk away from the people that cause you drama and know that it's their problem, not yours.

The days that you smile "just because," laugh because it feels good and dance because no one and every one is watching!

The days that you're overwhelmed by the kindness of strangers and believe that there truly is good in this world.

The days that you know that you made a positive difference in someone's life and in the world.

The days that you wake up grateful to have another day to live your best life.

The "some days" will happen now and again, but it's those "other days" that help us get through them and send them on their way.

I love those "other days."

Don't you?

"You Can't Always Get What You Want"

**"You can't always get what you want, but if you try
sometimes you just might find, you get what you need."
~The Rolling Stones~**

Life is all about making the best of what you have when you can't have things exactly the way that you want them, or when you can't have it "your" way but have to compromise with someone else, or when what you want just wasn't meant to be. No matter what, we don't always get what we want, and we have to learn to accept that and not hold onto the disappointment.

That's life. We want what we want, but sometimes circumstances prevent us from having it, so you have to make the best of what you have.

More often than not, you will always get what you need.

We want everything in our life to be as close to perfection as we can, but life isn't perfect and it isn't meant to be.

I understand that it's disappointing when we don't get what we want but that's not to say that there isn't something better that's meant to happen for us. After all, everything happens for a reason. People get sick, money runs out, the weather is horrible, you're too tired, and the list goes on. There are so many things that can prevent us from having what we want, but if you change your perspective on that, you'll find that you will get what you need.

What do you do when you don't get what you want? You accept that you didn't and change your perspective on it. Feel the disappointment, because that's a normal emotion, but don't let it ruin your day or night or life. Be careful that you're not ruining the time for someone else who may have been involved in what "you" wanted. Be spontaneous and accept that the plans changed and start making new ones! Make the best of the situation!

I can tell you that some of the best times I've had in my life happened when I didn't get what I wanted, but I always got what I needed, and that turned out to be an amazing experience or a chance to have or do something better than what I had hoped.

I'd be the first one to tell you that I don't always get what I want, sometimes I don't even get what I need, but I make the best of it. As I always say: "It won't be like this forever, just for today."

Lighten up, my friends. We don't always get what we want and unless it's life threatening to you or someone else, why waste your energy and your time getting upset over it? It's time that you'll never get back and it will be time you lost with the people you love.

Let it go.

Go with the flow.

Change your perspective.

Keep your mind open to all that the world has to offer you.

The possibilities are endless.

"UNCOMFORTABLE SITUATIONS"

I had an interesting conversation with my oldest son one night. We were talking about how we find ourselves in "uncomfortable situations." I told him I had just gone through a similar experience not long ago and so did he. We didn't tell one another the details but we had a long talk about it and understood what each of us were feeling.

I told him that my opinion was that it's the person that feels uncomfortable that needs to figure out why they are. He felt differently. His feeling was that someone who knows you well wouldn't put you in an uncomfortable situation. After all, most of us don't put ourselves in a situation in which we feel uncomfortable or out of place, unless we're growing and learning, which at times, can be uncomfortable. Most often times when we do find ourselves in those situations it's usually because someone put us in it.

My son proceeded to tell me that when one person puts another person in an uncomfortable situation, all the while knowing that the person feels that way, is because they have no empathy, compassion or respect for the feelings of the person they are with. He said that goes for friends or a significant other. I had to agree with him because it made perfect sense.

We as humans may have to do some uncomfortable things to step out of our comfort zone but rarely do we put ourselves in situations in which we feel uncomfortable, uneasy or out of place. Truth be told, if WE put ourselves in that position, then we're to blame but what if someone we love and care about puts us in that position? What does that say about how they feel about us? What does it say for how we feel about them?

It seems to me that if my friends or significant other puts me in that position then they're only concerned with their own feelings, definitely not mine, and if I allow them to put me in that position it's saying that I value their feelings more than my own. It seems like a slippery slope but it's not. If you love and care about someone you don't ever put them in a situation they're uncomfortable with, whether you understand their feelings or not. You respect them enough to avoid those situations and you respect their boundaries. Loving and caring about someone is putting their feelings above your own when these types of situations arise.

You see, life isn't that complicated but depending on the situation, people make it that way. I can promise the people that I love and care about that I will never put them in an uncomfortable situation and I would expect that they would do the same for me. In a perfect world, they would, but it's not a perfect world and some people do.

Be aware of the people in your life that dismiss your feelings because of their own selfish ways. They don't have to agree with your feelings or even understand why you're feeling that way, but they should respect them enough to keep you out of those situations.

If they don't, then you have a choice to make. They may not be your "people."

Anyone who puts someone that they care about in a situation that they know is uncomfortable for them has just let them know how important they are.

Be mindful of the feelings of the people you care about even when you don't understand them.

The situations you are not uncomfortable in may be the ones that they are.

Be respectful.

Decide what your priority is. Is it the person you care about or the situation?

The choice is yours and they have a choice as well.

Pay attention to their choice.

"Free Will"

I have a close circle of friends and there are moments that I sit and wonder why they make the choices that they do. I know to my toes that it may not be their best choice, but they make it anyway.

I bet, in all fairness, they think the same thing about my choices.

We love who we love and we love the people in our circle, yet there are moments that they're handed a situation in which they have to make a choice and sometimes those that love them sitting on the outside of it wonder why they chose the path that they did. We wonder why they made the decision that they did. We wonder what they were thinking that brought them to their decision.

We wonder if we should suddenly step in and tell them that we think that their decision is wrong, that we know they'll only be hurt by it in the end and that they should know that their decision is wrong.

We shouldn't.

We may feel that they're making the wrong decision, but it's at that moment that we need to step back and let them move forward with their choices, whether we believe them to be right or wrong.

It's their "free will," not ours.

I've learned that if we don't let them lead their own lives, make their own choices, and do what they think is right, then they'll never learn a lesson that their life is about to hand them.

That's "free will."

It's allowing those we love the freedom to make their own choices, even if our intuition tells us that it's wrong.

We learn life lessons by making mistakes and learning from them.

When someone takes away our free will, they've also taken away a valuable moment in our life. They've taken away our right to make a choice, good or bad, and learn from it.

We may not always understand why the ones we love make the choices that they do, but a big part of loving them is respecting them enough to allow them their free will to do so.

We all want to protect those that are important to us, but if we don't allow them to make their own choices and in some cases, mistakes, then we took away their right to learn and grow as a person.

The best thing we can do is to be there to support them if they should make the wrong choice and be there to celebrate with them when they make the right choice.

"The One Word I Despise: VICTIM"

I don't get angry very often and I try not to get upset at someone who says hurtful things to me, but I will tell you this, there is ONE WORD that will make my blood boil and fill me with an anger that makes my head spin: VICTIM! Aside from those emotions, it hurts my heart, because I'm not that and refuse to play the part.

I had an experience in which someone decided to call me that publicly. The comments were nasty, untrue, and bordering on "threatening" and they called me a "victim."

I am not a victim, I am a survivor and extremely proud of that.

I am a survivor of divorce, abuse and breast cancer. I never once saw myself as a victim of any of these things because, while I never wanted to have any of it happen, I accepted them as life lessons. Those things happened to me so that I could learn from them, survive them, and use my voice through my writing to help others going through those situations.

Me? A victim?

No, not by a long shot.

There are those that play the victim themselves. They are martyrs and portray themselves as good people, when in reality, they are quick to judge and despise anyone who has something they want. They are the ones who choose to play the victim so that they can get all the attention that they are desperately seeking.

Trust me, I'm not one of them.

I don't have a perfect life, but it's perfect for me. I have five beautiful children, all of whom I'm very proud of. I am able to pursue my passion of writing every day of my life. I'm surrounded by some amazing friends who always have my back and see me as a survivor. My "bubble" is filled with the people that support me and more importantly, love me.

None of them believe me to be a victim because they know I'm not.

I write about my past experiences in a positive light, hoping to let others know that they're not alone, that there's always hope, and there's always a way to get through it.

I know that there are people who will judge me, but if you're going to do that, make sure that you know me. Don't see me through the eyes of hatred and jealousy, see me through the eyes of "truth."

"Survivor" is one of my favorite words. It means you had enough faith in yourself and your Higher Power to get through the tough times. Life hasn't always been easy for me, yet I choose to be grateful for every day I wake up, for every experience that life hands me, be it good or bad. After all, in the end everything is a lesson to learn so that we can live our best life possible.

Once again, I'll remind you of this: "If you can't be kind, be quiet."

"Moments In Life"

There are moments in life that make you feel like your head is spinning and you can't get a handle on all that is going on around you. It's when that happens that you need to turn off the world for a little while. You need to take a step back from all that is happening around you and find a place of quiet in order to take a breath. These are the moments in which you need to turn off the radio and television, power down the computer and put your cell phone on silent.

The times you need to do this are the times when you need to do it for YOU!

Life can get crazy and "not so good" situations seem to arise, but it's important that we learn how to handle these times, how to distance ourselves from the stress and drama, and how to handle the uncertainties that life can throw at us.

We need to turn it all off for a bit so that we can re-energize ourselves and find the balance we need so that we can turn it back on.

Sometimes we need only the sounds of the birds chirping, or of the waves crashing on the shore. Sometimes we only need the sounds of nature, the feel of the warm sun shining on our face, or the touch of a gentle hand holding ours.

Sometimes all we need is some peace and quiet to collect our thoughts, to catch our breath, and to find our balance.

Sometimes we just need to turn off the world so that we can find our strength to turn it back on.

"When The Power Goes Out"

—◦◦❦◦◦—

We get some pretty intense storms during the summer months here at the Shore, the kind which most often leaves you without power! They are the storms filled with heavy winds, torrential downpours and occasionally, tornadoes. It seems as though we have such a storm that causes power outages at least once a season, and my family and I just experienced one of them.

It was about 6 pm on a Monday that a quick, but powerful, storm blew through our area. We lost power within seconds and it would turn out to be almost 30 hours before it was restored, and almost 40 hours for the internet to come back up. I lost one tree and part of another, but happy to say that we were all safe and sound, as were most of us in this area.

It was a crazy 40 hours, yet when you lose power and use of the internet, you begin to realize just how much you appreciate it. It's that old saying "you don't know what you have until it's gone." I took those 40 hours and tried to embrace them as well as I could. It was frustrating at first to know that the laundry was piling up from the weekend, that the cleaning I had hoped to get done on Tuesday just wasn't going to happen, and that I couldn't do much writing without the internet and my computer. The house was dark inside even during the day because the sun never came out and we sat under gray, overcast skies. We ate dinner that night by candlelight and found our way through the house with flashlights.

So, what did I do without electricity? I decided to be grateful for the time without my daily responsibilities and do something I haven't done in forever: read a book instead of writing one! I took my tablet and sat outside where it was a bit brighter and much cooler and began reading. I felt guilty at first for not getting certain things done, yet I realized that this was a time to change things up, relax, read, sit outside, talk on the phone and catch up with old friends. I had the gift of doing anything I wanted to do that didn't involve electricity!

It truly was the "sweetness of doing nothing," and while I'm happy that our power is back on and the internet is back up, it was somewhat of a gift to spend my day in a much different way than usual.

**"Don't wait for circumstances that force
you to do something different.
Create the circumstances that allow you to do something different."**

"Put It Down and Shut It Off"

———❦———

In this day and age most everyone has a cell phone, a social media page, and a computer. Let's face it, it's the way the world is today. We search, we follow, we like, we comment...it's all part of the world of technology we live in. In fact, most of us are lost without it, and that is both a true statement and sad fact.

I'll be the first to admit that I have a cell phone, social media pages and a laptop. My career revolves around them, yet I try to be disciplined about the times I am using them. It's important to know when to be on them and when to turn them off.

The time to turn them off is when I'm having human interaction, whether it's with my friends or family, my significant other, or even a stranger. I know that my time with the people I love is precious and not promised. I guess you could say that my time with social media, the internet and cell phones is ALWAYS promised as long as I pay the bill!

The truth is that our lives are not promised. We all know how precious a human life is and it frustrates me beyond belief that some people don't get that. So often they say they do get that until they're on the phone, or social media, or their computer.

I feel unimportant and disrespected when someone, be it my significant other, family, child or friend is in my presence and on the phone checking social media. It's one thing if it's work but it's another when it's pleasure. I feel hurt at thinking that I'm not as important to them as their social media, phone or computer. Let's face it, we can check our social media anytime we want. Posts and comments can be there forever, but I'm not and you're not. No one is.

Most people don't even realize how long they're looking at their social media because they go into this "hyper-focus" mode. They lose track of time and more importantly, they lose sight of the person sitting with them. They forget what's important to them, then again, maybe the "likes, comments and views" of others on social media are more important to them than the "likes, comments or views" of the person that they're with.

I feel that if you can sit on your phone, internet or social media that long while I'm with you, then you've just let me know what's more important to you and it's not me.

Always remember that the time you spend on social media, the phone or the computer while you are with the ones you love is time that you can't get back. Would you rather spend 15 minutes on the internet or 15 minutes with someone important to you?

Life is short, the internet is long.

You decide what and who is more important.

Think about that.

Put down the cell phone and turn off the electronics when you're with the people you love.

The "likes and loves" you receive from them will last a lifetime.

"Busy Making A Living"

Let's face it, we need money to survive. We have to pay the bills, the rent or the mortgage, put food on the table and keep clothes on our backs. We need money to do these things and most of us will do what it takes to do that for our families. We work full-time or part-time and take the overtime that's offered to us. We work and we work and we work to do all those things, those "responsible" things.

On the other hand, how much do we need? Do we need all those things that we work so hard to get? Is there a balance between what we have to do to make a living to afford all those things or do we do what we have to do to make a life to spend time with the people we're busy making a living for?

There's a quote that reads like this: "Don't get so busy making a living that you forget to have a life."

It's an important thought to think about.

I know it's important to be able to make a living, but more often than not, I see people so busy and exhausted making that living that there's nothing left of them to enjoy the life it affords or the people that they love who support them to make that living.

Do we work until exhaustion because of our ego and self-esteem? Do you feel like "more of a man" when you work more than 40 hours a week? Does it make you feel like more of an "empowered woman" when you work all week and on weekends? Is all that work outside of what is really necessary about our self-esteem?

We seem to live in a society that is built upon making money and "having it all," yet I've seen a shift in society as well. Everyone is working more than normal but looking for answers as to why their life seems to be missing something. They feel a void, fatigue, and moments of "is this is as good as it gets.?"

No one is asking you to spend 50 or 60 hours a week working yourself to death to pay for the unnecessary things in life because you put that pressure on yourself. No one is asking you to work until the point of exhaustion so that you can't enjoy your life filled with family or friends because you made that choice. No one is asking you to get so busy making a living that you don't have the time or energy to have a life because you made that decision.

Life doesn't go on forever, and neither does the job or career. In fact, the job and career most often times will end long before the life does.

Life is short, precarious, and unsure.

We're not promised another day and we're not promised a job.

We're not promised time and we're not promised job security.

We're not promised that our loved ones will always be there and we're not promised that the job will either.

The people who love us want to spend time with us whereas the job wants us to spend time working.

The people who care about us want us to be well and happy and enjoy life while the job wants us to be well and happy so that we can do their work.

The people we are making a life with want that life to be filled with memories while the job only wants that your life be filled with hours that don't make a memory, but fill a quota.

The people you love are the life and the job is just a living.

The people who love you don't lay you off or replace you for someone better but the job will.

The people who love you want to spend time with you while the job wants you to spend time working overtime.

The people who love you don't need anything from you, they simply want what's good FOR you, while the job wants what they can get FROM you.

The people who love you, RESPECT you, and care about your well-being will understand when you say "no" to them because they know that you're feeling exhausted or need some down time. The job doesn't take "no" for an answer because they don't respect you or care about your well-being.

Life is short and no day is promised and neither is the job. So, while you need to make a living to pay the bills, don't forget to make a "life" while you're doing it.

Make the life you want and deserve with people that appreciate you, love you, and are part of that "life" you are living.

In the end, the job won't be there to take care of you if you're hurt, or understand if you're too exhausted to work overtime and the job won't care if something happens to you because they'll find someone else to replace you.

The ones who love you will always care because they know that you can't be replaced.

"Making a life" is all about surrounding yourself with the people who love you and about enjoying everyday and every moment with them. It's about making memories and of hearts taking pictures.

Don't get so busy making a living that you forget to have a life.

Learn to say "no" when you need to.

Say "yes" when you want to.

It's a good thing.

"Losing The Time You'll Never Get Back"

I want to give you something to think about. Think about all the countless hours you spend working for a living and all the countless hours you lose spending time with the people you love. Now, think about this: you will never get that time back again.

I'm blessed to have a career that allows me to work at home, and believe me when I say that it's work, but it's work that I love. One thing I know for sure is that I will never get so busy writing, editing, marketing or making phone calls that I forget to make time with the ones I love. My career would mean nothing to me if that were the case. I love the time I spend writing, but I love my time with the important people in my life much more.

I've worked 9-5 jobs throughout my life, yet I still held to one important fact: I love my job (most of the time) but I love my life and the people in it much more. It's a balancing act of knowing when to say "no" to overtime and a time to decide what and who your priority is: your job or your life. I've always chosen the people in my life because I realized that neither the job nor the people in my life will always be there, so I had to choose which was more important, and I did.

I'm going to go out on a limb here and tell you where this story came from and it comes from a place of love. It's a tough position for me to be in, yet being the person I am, I needed to figure out a way to explain my feelings and more importantly, how this situation was looking to me and to the outside world.

So, I realized what the most important part of this was: the person I care about was losing precious time to someone who didn't care about him and he was giving his time away to someone who didn't deserve it. All that time was given in vain and he will never get that time back again, not with me, his friends, or his family.

It was born from an experience from me watching someone I care about work more hours than he was meant to, deserved to, or wanted to. He kept telling his "boss" that he was exhausted and needed a day off, yet his boss didn't seem to care. He wanted what he wanted and he got it at the expense of someone I care about and all of us in his life. This person worked every weekend he was off and he's worked on every day that he was supposed to be off. He's worked more overtime than was necessary or what I believed to be humanly possible because the other employees in the office didn't want to do the work. I have to admit, this was upsetting to me because no one wants to watch someone they care about worn down and beaten into submission to do what someone else wanted them to do. No one wants to be spending time together with the one they care about on a weekend with the phone constantly spitting out text noises from a boss who wants more and more and more from him and wouldn't stop until he got what he wanted and wouldn't leave them alone until he did. No one wants to watch someone they care about feel less of who they are because of someone who feels more of who they are by using their power and position to feel "in control."

I've lost so many people I've loved over the past few years and while I know they're at peace now, I wish I had more time with them.

This is the point that I'm trying to make by writing this article: be mindful of the person you spend your precious time on and with and be mindful of the people you take it away from.

As we get older we understand more and more how precarious and unpredictable life really is. We learn to appreciate how short and precious life really is.

Take a look at your life, your job and at the amount of time you spend on each of them.

Take a look at the most important people in your life who love and respect you.

Take a look at the people you allow to control you and the ones who make you feel small.

Decide who you want to spend your precious time with.

Decide who you want to give the time to.

Decide who you don't want to give the time to.

The choice is yours as to where and who you spend your time with.

Please think about it, be mindful of it and choose it wisely because time wasted on the wrong people is time that is lost on the right people for a lifetime.

No one should live with regret over having spent time with anything or anyone that is less important than the people who are.

Shower the people you love with love.

Don't worry about the ones that you don't.

> **"The time you give to the wrong people is the time you lose from the right people and you'll never get that time back."**

"Take The Time"

If I've learned one important thing in life, it's this: when I find myself thinking about someone, I'm going to reach out to them to let them know that they were on my mind.

After all, wouldn't you want to know if someone is thinking of you? It means a lot to know that you crossed someone's mind and they took the time to let you know. It's easy to say "I thought of you all day" or "you've been on my mind lately," yet it's another thing to back those statements up with actions to prove that you really did. After all, as I always say, it's the actions that make the words true.

I can't begin to tell you how much it means to me to get a private message, text, or better yet, a phone call from someone who begins the conversation with: "I've been thinking of you and wanted to see how you're doing," or "I've missed you," or "you crossed my mind today and I wanted to let you know that I love you or that I just wanted to hear your voice."

It's those moments in which someone reached out to me that mean the world to me, and I know it means a lot to the people in my life that I take the time to do that for. No day is promised and I want to be sure that when someone crosses my mind I let them know that they did.

We're human and we all want to know that we're loved, or that we're needed, or that we're appreciated or thought of throughout the day, the night, or every now and again. It's those moments of someone letting us know that they thought of us is what keeps us going and makes us feel good, feel loved, feel happy. It's what makes us want to do the same for others.

Who did you reach out to today? Did you let someone important to you know how you feel about them? Did you take a moment to let someone know that you were thinking of them? Did you stop for a moment during your day to let someone know that you love them or thinking of them? I hope that you did.

Who reached out to you today? I hope someone did.

"It's the actions that make the words you say to someone true."

"Nothing Can Be Everything"

Did you ever realize that in order to take the day off, spend it doing nothing and turn the world off, we need to make a conscious decision to give ourselves permission to do so?

Did you ever find yourself, at the end of the day, thinking "I didn't get anything that I wanted to do done today," and then you feel frustrated and angry with yourself?

I've had those days and I did make a "conscious decision" to forget all those questions and ways of thinking.

Why did I do that?

It's because I've come to accept that some days I'm tired and don't have the energy to get everything on my "to do" list done, or that I've run out of time to fulfill all my commitments and responsibilities that day or that some days I just don't feel like doing anything.

I've learned that on the days I feel like I'm doing "nothing" I'm actually doing "everything."

That is, everything that is important for "me."

I'm resting, recuperating and re-energizing my mind, body and soul and sometimes I think it takes more effort to shut ourselves down than it does to run around like a crazy person! Think about it: we've been taught to believe that unless we've done all that we need to do in a day we're not doing anything.

I've had people ask me: "What did you do all day?"

My answer is usually this: "Not much of anything and while it may seem like nothing to you, it was everything to me."

I know we all have responsibilities in our lives, but we have to realize that it's okay to have that time for ourselves in order to be the best person we can be.

Next time you get to the end of the day and feel like you haven't accomplished what you wanted to, ask yourself this: "Did you accomplish taking care of yourself? Did you enjoy having a day off and the most important question, do you feel better?"

It's moments of doing nothing that are actually our best moments of doing everything.

"Here Comes Bulk Day"

There's one day every month that is my favorite and it's BULK DAY! It's during the warmer months that are the perfect time to spend the day hauling things that are no longer of value out to the curb. And I love getting rid of all that clutter!

My son and I spent all day a few days before "bulk day" going through the garage and basement. We hauled out one item after another. I find the whole process therapeutic. Some people are emotional eaters, I'm an emotional cleaner!

My kids and I function much better with less clutter in the house, garage, and basement. In fact, most people I know function better without clutter.

As for me, cleaning is an emotional process and I'm not talking about the everyday type of cleaning. I'm talking about the nitty gritty "organize the spice rack and clean out the closets" type of cleaning. It's such a great feeling to get rid of stuff. It gives you more space and it gives you more time to do the things you want to do or to simply do "nothing" without guilt!

Your home and your mind are your "sacred space," that place where you can be yourself, enjoy peace, and live on love. Clearing out your home is just as important as clearing out your mind and your mind can hold clutter as well.

Clear out the clutter of stress and drama, especially when it doesn't belong to you.

Clear out the clutter of negative thoughts.

Clear out the clutter of toxic people surrounding you.

The more you clear out ALL the types of clutter, the more space you open up for all good and positive things to come into your home, your mind, and your life.

You'll be glad that you did.

I know that I am.

"Respect And Social Media"

✦

Social media is one of the greatest inventions that there is, and also one of the worst when used in the wrong way. I've been researching and watching social media for years and the bottom line is this: Is there respect on the internet? So often I see boundaries crossed on social media that wouldn't be crossed in the real world. I see people portray themselves as something that they're not and you engage with someone who is not their authentic self.

This is when **"social networking" becomes "social NOTworking."**

It's how trust is lost in a friendship or relationship, it's how affairs begin, and it's how we lose ourselves in a fantasy world of being someone we're not.

It's how we get away with disrespecting other people, such as the significant other or spouse of the people we know, friends or family.

I've been on the other side of people disrespecting me through my significant other, my friends, and my family using social media as their method of doing it.

It's not fair because they only care about their own selfish gratification of getting a "like" or "comment" from someone they have no real contact or relationship with. I often wonder if it's because they're so unhappy in their own relationships that they want to cause trouble in someone else's. I wonder why any decent and kind human being would want to cause a problem for someone else.

Personally, I've had enough.

I look at the world around me, a world that at times is filled with tragedy, loss, and sadness. I read about people who lost their lives and loved ones in fires, from shootings, or who suffer a personal pain on a daily basis and it saddens me. We could be using social media to help someone, not hurt them. We could be using it to make a difference in the life of another or in the world. We could be using it to lift someone's spirits or let them know we care about them. We could use it for so many positive things, yet there are people who won't.

They are the people that are unhappy in their own lives that they want to make someone else just as unhappy. They are the ones who want to ruin someone else's relationship because they don't have one or aren't content in the one they're in. They are the ones who stalk people just to make their life miserable. They are the ones that spread hate, judgement, and negativity on social media. There's enough abuse in the real world, why become abusive on social media?

Seriously, we all have to get back to living among the living.

Let's get back to being kind and compassionate to each other. Let's be respectful of the lives of others, be it their relationships, family or friends. The world on social media should be lived just as you would in the real, physical world: honestly, respectfully and with kindness.

Take accountability in your life and in your life on social media.

Be as respectful on social media as you would in person.

Don't cause havoc in the relationships of others just because you think you can on social media.

Let social media be a place to share positivity, to make someone laugh, or to change the world.

Think before you like.

Think before you comment.

Think before you post.

I believe that there can be respect on social media, but the choice is all yours.

I hope you choose wisely.

"Happiness Or Having A Good Time?"

This is certainly a topic that's made a few people I know think about this question: "Are you really happy?" They tell me they are happy based on their ability to have a good time when they're out in social situations, but I say that it's not the same.

I think that being "happy" is not the same as "having a good time."

Let me explain.

Let's be honest, when most of us are in social situations we're under the influence of something. For example, most people I know are all happy when they're out drinking but that's not happy, that's having a good time.

What about when you're not under the influence of anything other than a clear, sober mind? Are you happy? Are you able to feel joy or are you counting the days until the next social situation in which you can numb your reality and feelings? Those are the questions you need to ask yourself. It's definitely worth standing in your truth about.

I'm not judging anyone, I'm simply observing the behavior of others.

I may not always have a great day but I can tell you that I'm happy everyday. It may not look like it to those around me, but my heart is happy that I woke up in the morning and was gifted another day of life to make a difference in the world.

I'm a girl that loves a glass or two of wine, yet I know I don't need it to be happy. I feel happiness without it. I don't allow it to become more important than the people in my life. There is nothing that would make me lose sight of the ones I love.

Are you happy or are you only happy when you're having a good time and under the influence of something other than a clear mind?

Think about it.

"Don't Just Sit There... Do Something"

I can remember a time or two when my children were younger that they would come home with a story about one child being a bully to another. I asked them, "That's not nice to do to someone. What did you do?" They looked at me and said, "Nothing. They weren't doing it to me."

Bam! Here comes a learning lesson from mom. I sat them down and explained a few things to them. Funny thing is, what I told them way back then is still true today, even as adults.

I told them that if they don't try to help then they're just as bad as the bully because they should have at least tried to protect the child being bullied.

It was a simple lesson and an important lesson, yet I see some adults that never learned that.

I always felt, and tried to teach my children this, that you have to try to help someone who's being treated badly or being hurt. You may not always succeed in stopping the situation, but at least you didn't sit back and do nothing. It's when you do nothing that you become as guilty as the person doing the bad thing because you're lack of actions to stop it is confirmation to all those around that the bad behavior is okay. You're saying that you don't see anything wrong with someone being hurt.

I understand that there are situations in which we may get physically hurt trying to stop it, yet there are other things someone can do. If you're in school, go to the principal or tell your teacher. If you're living next door to a home in which there is abuse happening, call the police. There's always something that can be done to try and help.

It upsets me when I'm the one on the receiving end of an "adult bully" and the people that claim to care about me sit and watch it happening. They don't do anything to stop it or correct the other person. They seem to believe that the best way to handle it is to ignore it and let it go.

I get it but try being the one bullied. When someone is treating me badly it hurts my heart and what hurts even more is when the people I love and care about do nothing to stop it. They don't open their mouth and they just sit there wishing it away.

Thank you. You've just let me know my worth and you let the bully know that they have all the worth. You've let them know that their bad behavior is acceptable. You've let them know that they can keep doing it without accountability. You've let them win over someone like me that did nothing to them and didn't deserve it.

I've always told my children that there are no "bad people," just "bad behavior," and that's true with a bully.

They lack self-esteem and are filled with insecurities and jealousy. They seek attention and want to feel important.

When you sit there and do nothing, you've just given them the attention and importance they desire but don't deserve.

Don't just sit there. Do something.

Your "something" could be just what they need to turn their "bad behavior" into "good behavior."

CHAPTER SEVEN

"A Breath About Relationships"

"Where Is The Love?"

There's so much craziness out there in the world and in our personal lives that we have to ask ourselves this question: "Where is the love?"

I don't know where it's hiding, but I know that we all have it within us and it's our choice to share it or not.

It's easier to love than to hate.

It's easier to be kind than be cruel.

It's easier to listen than to ignore.

It's easier to understand than be ignorant.

It's easier to be compassionate than be cold.

It's easier to hug than to hurt.

It's easier to say I'm sorry than to say you're always right.

It's easier to forgive than it is to hold a grudge.

It's easier to take accountability than it is to lay blame.

It's easier to be open-minded than close minded.

I may be a simple minded girl when it comes to love, but I do know that every negative emotion or action will never bring anything positive into your life or the life of anyone else.

We don't always understand or agree with one another but there is so much more to be gained when we take the time to try and understand the feelings of another person rather than always blame them and tell them they're wrong. There's more to learn when we try to see the perspective of another person.

The only way you can do this is with an open heart, one that is filled with love, kindness, and compassion.

You don't need to do those things if you're a perfect person.

As far as I know, no one person is perfect and if they think that they're always right and that everyone else is wrong, then they have my sympathy because they're wrong. They take their insecurities about themselves out on those that are just seeking kindness from another human being.

Kindness counts.

Love counts.

Listening to others counts.

Compassion counts.

Truth and honesty count.

The world can be a crazy place and crisis seems to be everywhere, yet if we all are on the same page of love and kindness we can change that, make it easier, and make a difference.

Let's change this world together, one day, one step, one person at a time.

Be kind, my friends.

Be compassionate.

Be loving to others.

Be respectful and don't judge the lives of others because you don't always know what they're going through.

Be a human being that can change a life and the world for the better.

Are you with me on this? Are you ready to make a difference in this world together?

I am.

Let's do this together.

"I Want To Know What Love Is"

Do you want to know how the people in your life really feel about you? I think I figured how and I learned it through my own personal experience.

"Speak your truth, voice your opinion without judgement, and tell them how you feel."

If they accept your truth and don't get angry or defensive, then they're listening to you with their heart.

If they get angry at you and start telling you that you're wrong and all the things that they think are wrong with you, then they're listening with their ego.

It's called projection.

"Projection is the inability to take accountability."

I know projection all too well. I've been on the other side of it more times than I can count, but all those times taught me how to recognize it. I can see it coming a mile away.

Projection happens when you speak your truth to someone and they don't like it because they know you're right and they're wrong, and they haven't learned the finer points of saying "I'm sorry" and meaning it.

No one likes to be told that they hurt the feelings of someone they love, but personally, if you truly, down to your toes, love someone, you'll listen and you'll listen with your heart. Not everyone hurts someone they love intentionally. Sometimes it happens because of miscommunication between two people, and that's forgivable, understandable and acceptable.

When you hurt someone intentionally and don't apologize and take accountability for the feelings that your behavior caused them, then it's hard to forgive, understand and accept.

I don't like to know that I hurt someone, especially since I wouldn't hurt anyone I care about intentionally, but if I do, I'm the first to apologize and say that I didn't realize it had hurt their feelings. I'll ask them if there's anything I can do to ease the pain I caused.

Not everyone can do that.

It's because the ego doesn't like to be wrong.

The heart accepts when it's wrong.

That's how you learn to see what true love between significant others, family and friends is about.

It's listening, accepting, understanding, and saying you're sorry.

The ego says "I'm always right and you're always wrong." End of discussion.

The heart says "I'm so sorry, I never meant to hurt you, let's fix this," and that's how you know who really loves you and means it.

Love is the greatest emotion in the world yet there are so many people who use the word without knowing what it truly means, what it entails, and what amazing things it can do.

Love is kind, beautiful, and has the ability to last forever.

Love is simple, honest, and forgiving.

I've been loved by the heart and loved by the ego in this lifetime of mine so far, and I can tell you this, being loved by the heart is the best. It's truth, it's compassion, it's loyalty, and it has the ability to last forever.

When you are loved by the ego, it's not based on truth, doesn't know how to be compassionate and is never truly loyal. This type of life will never last a lifetime.

All I ever wanted to know in my lifetime is what love really is.

I know what it is and I've learned to know what it isn't.

I know this because I love the people in my life with my heart, not with an ego.

Be mindful of how you love someone and how they love you. Love from your heart.

"LOVE AND RELATIONSHIPS"

I've learned a thing or two about love and relationships throughout my life. I've learned that you have to feel the love someone has for you in order to know that they really do love you.

Sounds simple, right?

You would think so, but it's not always as simple as we would like it to be.

Love shouldn't be complicated and I've always believed that it's the people involved that make it complicated, yet my feelings on that have changed slightly over the years.

It's true that people can make love complicated but I understand now why they do: we all speak in a different love language. What one person wants or needs to feel that love is not necessarily what the other person involved wants or needs.

"Love language" is all about what we need and how we want to be loved.

You could be in an amazing relationship, yet there is still a difference in each person's "love language." For some, it's as simple as being taken care of and more about the "physical" stuff, while for others it's deeper than that, it's the emotional.

I'm a "hopeful" romantic, so my love language is simple. I need to know I'm thought of, appreciated and accepted for who I am. I need and want the little things: flowers, a love note, or a simple act of romance and kindness for me.

There are others that need and want more of the physical aspects: they need to have their meals cooked for them, laundry done, and their needs taken care of.

That's two very different love languages, two very different people, but can it work?

It can, but both people need to understand and accept the "love language" of the other and want to fill to fill those needs and wants.

You need to love that person enough to fill those needs and wants without complaining about them.

The simple truth of love is this: if you really love someone you will fill their "love tank."

The best sign of love is when you're willing to give them that which may mean nothing to you and they're willing to do the same.

What if you can't? I would say that you're not in love with them, you're in love with love.

We grow from love, we don't gain from it.

Isn't the love we grow together as a couple the best love of all?

I think so.

"TRUST"

"Trust." It isn't just about cheating anymore.

Maybe it never was.

Trust encompasses so many dynamics and I'm talking about the trust in relationships.

I have my own personal opinion on trust. It's how I know I'm safe in a relationship to trust the other person with all that I am.

Here are my thoughts on this.

In a relationship you have to trust that the other person will:

Always be open and honest with you and never lie.

Have your back at all times.

Listen to you talk about your feelings, try to understand them, and not judge them.

Never yell at your for being who you are.

Mean it when they say that they love you and will have the actions to make the words true.

Always be kind and cherish you.

Know your value.

Accept you for who you are.

Help you through a difficult time.

Never hurt your heart.

Take accountability for their actions, especially if they hurt you.

Communicate with you when there's a problem

Make you their priority.

Let you know that you're important.

Never take you for granted.

Appreciate all that you do for them.

Defend you and not the person who hurt you.

Make time for you.

Put in the effort when needed.

Be your best friend.

Love you the way you need to be loved.

Trust.

It's not just about trusting they won't cheat on you.

It's knowing that they are your safety net to be who you are.

It's love.

Pure and simple.

"Trust And Vulnerability"

I believe that the most important trust is the one in which you trust someone with your heart, your soul and your feelings. It's trusting that they won't hurt the heart that you've so willingly given to them. It's trusting that they won't belittle your feelings or get angry with you for having them.

It's trusting them with your vulnerability.

When they react hurtfully to that vulnerability, the trust is broken.

How can you be in a relationship or friendship with anyone that takes advantage of your trust in them? How many times can you keep giving them your heart only to have the same response and reaction each time? How many times will you believe so much in them that you believe that the next time will be different?

The one time that someone hurts you when you're trusting them with your heart and feelings is the time to open your eyes and accept that you can't trust them. Accept that the person you thought they were isn't that person at all. Accept that believing with all your heart that they'll change the next time you're vulnerable will never happen.

People are who they are. Some are kind and selfless, some are mean and selfish.

You have a choice of who you surround yourself with. It's not healthy to be in any relationship in which you don't feel "safe" to share your heart, your mind and your feelings.

We all have a choice to be kind, considerate, non-judgemental, loving, respectful, selfless, understanding, considerate and compassionate to others.

We have a choice to apologize to someone we hurt, forgive someone who hurt us, and to make things right when things go wrong.

We all have a choice to go to bed angry or make peace with the person that we're angry with, to take our accountability or blame others, and to accept our shortcomings or project them onto someone else.

Unfortunately, not everyone will choose to be that way or do those things.

You can and I hope that you do.

"It Takes Effort"

I had a discussion with a friend of mine. He was saying that men (and he's a man) try to avoid discussions with a woman when they know they did something wrong or hurt their feelings. I said (as most women would) that ignoring the situation only makes it worse.

I believe that it does and I don't think it matters if you're male or female.

When you ignore someone's feelings, it makes them feel as if you don't care about them, and truth be told, if you do care about them you'd wouldn't want them to feel that way in the first place. It seems pretty simple to me. I always say that "love and relationships aren't complicated, it's the people involved in them that make it complicated."

I don't believe that relationships take work. I believe that they take effort from both people. It's putting in the effort to really know and understand the other person: how they think, what they like and don't like, what makes them happy and what upsets them. It's putting in the effort to make each other feel like a priority, not an option. It's putting in the effort to help one another, support one another, and be there for one another. It's putting in the effort to love, respect and cherish one another in the way each person needs to feel those things. What feeling "loved" means to one person may be different for the other, and that's okay as long as you put in the effort to understand what it is that makes them feel loved. It's putting in the effort to accept them for who they are and that includes the good and the bad. It's putting in the effort to learn how to communicate with one another.

It's putting in the effort to support your words with the action's that make them true.

Do you think about them when you're not together? Make the effort to send them a text or make a phone call to let them know that you are.

Do you appreciate all that they do for you? Make the effort to tell them as often as you can how much your appreciate them.

Do you see yourself living your life without them? Make the effort to be sure you don't lose them.

Do you like seeing them upset or hurt? Make the effort to find out why and help them get through it.

It's all about the effort because "effort is the best indicator of interest."

Don't let the ones you love feel like an option because you make everyone else a priority.

Don't let the ones you love feel as though they don't matter and everyone else does.

Don't let the ones you love feel ignored or taken for granted.

The effort you put into your relationship will be time well spent.

It could be the difference between a relationship lasting a short-time or one to last a lifetime.

The choice is yours.

"Boundaries"

It's important to set healthy boundaries in your life. They're the lines we put around our sacred space to be sure that no one crosses them. They're boundaries of what we will allow from others and what we won't.

Yet, boundaries aren't just for us, they're also for protecting what's important in our relationships.

If you respect your relationships then the boundaries you set protect them as well as they protect you.

I value my sacred space and my relationships as well. I try to set healthy boundaries for myself and my relationships so that the people in my life know that they're a priority, are important to me, and that I value them enough to prevent others from crossing them.

It also sends a powerful message to those that try and cross those boundaries.

There are some people that are selfish enough to consistently try and cross your boundaries. They don't care about the people in your life and more importantly, they don't care about you. They care about what they want and getting what they want.

There is only one person that can stop someone from crossing your boundaries and that person is YOU! After all, what you allow will continue.

Stop allowing people to disrespect your boundaries because when you allow them to do so, it will not only affect your life but the lives of the people you love.

Each time you let them cross your boundaries you're sending a clear message to your loved ones that those people matter more than they do. Love yourself and the people in your life enough to set healthy boundaries.

Set your priorities of what and who is most important to you. Set healthy boundaries around in your life.

Start saying "NO" to people who continually try to cross them.

After all, "NO" is a full sentence.

"Communication, Compromise and Consideration"

"Don't give in, give up. Change your direction."

At one time or another we find ourself in a situation that's missing three vital pieces: communication, compromise and consideration. No matter how hard we try to express our feelings to someone, they don't, can't or won't understand. They hear things the way that they want to hear them. The people involved in any relationship have to learn to communicate with one another without judgment. They have to be able to express their feelings openly and honestly without being told that they're wrong. They have to be respectful to each other and they have to feel safe to be their authentic-self with each other.

Sometimes that doesn't work.

What do you do when that happens? Do you give in and become the person that they want you to be?

No.

You don't give in anymore, you face a hard truth that things won't change and that you have to give up trying to make things work. There are some issues in a relationship that can't be resolved and giving in to try and make it work for one person is unfair. It's unfair to the person who has to give in.

You give up trying to fix or save a relationship after you've done everything in your power to find a resolution or compromise to make it work. It has to be both people willing to work on things and no one should give in. The time may come when both people have to give up on the relationship and move on.

Relationships cannot survive on love alone. It has to be two people loving each other enough to make things work, to communicate, and to understand one another. Both people have to be willing to compromise and they have to be considerate of each others feelings. It doesn't matter if it's a friendship or a romantic relationship, it's all the same.

If two people can't communicate with one another, then it's time to give up.

This is one time I will use the term "give up," because where relationships are concerned, you have to work together to make it work. If you're the one who is constantly "giving in" and always working on a problem with no resolution, then you're missing out on actually living your life. The problems in the relationship begin to overshadow your life and you end up feeling negative emotions.

Both people need to work together to make things work, yet sometimes the relationship just wasn't meant to work out.

The endings of relationships can be painful, especially when you don't want it to end, but you have to love yourself enough to BE your authentic self. Don't settle for less than you deserve because we all deserve good things.

You can't live your best life in a relationship that is filled with "giving in."

"Give up" trying to fix something that can't be fixed, trying to change who you are so that it will work, and trying to find a resolution that never comes.

It's time to change your direction.

It's time to live your best life.

"There's No Excuse To Lie"

There's no excuse to lie to someone, unless you have a spectacular surprise planned for them. Other than there, there's no excuse for it.

There's no such thing as a "small" lie. A lie is a lie and once it's told and the truth is found out, the trust is shattered.

The trust is hard to earn back once it does.

Trust must be earned and maintained, especially in relationships.

I've always said that I'd rather be hurt by the truth than disrespected by a lie.

I often wonder why people lie. Wouldn't it be easier to simply tell someone the truth? You know that in time the truth will always come out, and when it does, someone inevitably gets hurt.

I believe that people lie because they know the ramifications of telling the truth, so they lie. They lie because they're doing something that they know will upset someone, yet do it anyway, and then they lie about it. They lie because they're insecure and lying gives them a sense of power and control. They lie because they don't value honesty yet expect it from others.

They lie because they get away with it and don't seem to feel bad about it.

Most often, when the truth comes out to the person that they lied to, they get angry at the person. Why? Because they have no reason for the lie and want to turn it around on the innocent victim in the situation that THEY created.

The thing about lying is this: once you lie to someone, you open the door for them to wonder what else you've lied about and how long you have been lying to them.

Trust is broken and shattered and it's up to the person who lied to try and earn it back.

It's also up to the person that they lied to allow them a chance to earn it back.

Sometimes the trust is so badly broken that it can't be earned back.

The person who lied will never be fully trusted again and as my significant other always says to me: "If there's no trust in a relationship, then there's no real relationship."

He's right.

When you lie to someone you claim to love and care about, you've just told them that there are bigger priorities than them and that you didn't respect them enough to be honest with them.

Is that what you want?

Do you want them to lie to you?

Are you lying intentionally to hurt them?

Were you doing something wrong and didn't want them to know?

Think before you lie.

Think before you lie to the one you love.

Think before you lie to yourself.

"Words Aren't Always Good Enough"

I know the power of words and they have the ability to do so many things. They can hurt, heal, break a heart and make a heart soar. Words can end something and begin something new. They can change the world and another life. They can also destroy them both.

Words.

Powerful. Important. Necessary.

Yet, sometimes words aren't enough. Sometimes what we say has to be backed up by the actions that make them true.

Sometimes words can't explain, fix, heal or help someone to understand.

We can say the perfect words to express our needs and wants to another, yet that doesn't mean that they will be met.

That can be difficult to accept, whether it's a friendship or relationship.

We can love someone with all that we are, but if there's no understanding of the words that are spoken between both people it's usually the beginning of the end.

This is true with friends as well.

There are times that we have to stop trying so hard to communicate with someone. The truth is that perhaps the other person can't or doesn't want to understand what we're saying or that they just don't care enough to understand.

When the right words don't seem to help, we rely on the love we have for each other, yet that's not always enough either. Communication is the key in any relationship.

The two people in a relationship or friendship have to accept and realize that the relationship or friendship has served its time and taught them the lessons that they needed to learn. Words can't always solve a problem with a resolution between two people who care for one another.

The only time words are good enough is when the actions make them truth.

"It's Them, Not You"

There's this one life lesson that I'm obviously not learning as well as I should have and it snuck up on me again without warning. I was more angry at myself for allowing it to happen than I was at the person who did it.

I allowed someone to take out their insecurities, jealousies, and bad day on me by bringing up my painful past situations and mistakes that I've made peace with, moved on with, and learned from. I began defending myself throughout the conversation and I know better than to do that.

I felt completely drained by the time we hung up the phone. They had said so many hurtful things to me that I went to bed in tears, feeling like a failure.

The next day I woke up with a headache, a bruised heart, and a sadness in my soul, but I'm working on that. I know I'm not a failure because I'm living my life purpose and pursuing my passion and dreams. I know I'm not a failure because I keep moving forward with a positive attitude, despite what life or another person hands me and that I would never do anything hurtful to another person even though they did it to me.

I understand that people have bad days. I have them as well, but I would never take it out on another person. I taught my children to understand that when people are unkind, mean or hurtful to you, it's not really because of YOU, they are simply taking their fears, insecurities, jealousies or bad days out on you. They're afraid to face their own truth and their own life so they inflict emotional and verbal pain on you. It's not okay for anyone to do that to another human being. We can all understand why they do it, but we do NOT have to allow them to do it.

Are you wondering why I allowed this person to speak to me that way? It's because it was was someone in my family and I didn't see the conversation going in the direction that it did. I couldn't seem to shut it down no matter what I said.

I told my best friend about it and she said to me: "You should have turned around and spoken to them the same way they spoke to you and you should have treated them the same way."

My response: "I won't lower myself to that level and I will not be unkind to someone even if they're being unkind to me."

I believe that's a lesson for all of us. What we allow will continue and sometimes the people that are unkind to us are the closest to us, yet I believe this to be true: even if it's family, it's no reason to allow that type of bad behavior. Sometimes, especially with family, we have to wish them love and light and put some distance between us. It's difficult to do at times, but absolutely necessary.

Distance between family members doesn't mean you don't love them, it means you love yourself just as much.

My heart began to heal when I forgave them for speaking to me in that way and when forgave myself for allowing it.

"Be Careful What Door You Open"

Everyone has a past and each one is different. Some are filled with beautiful memories and some with heartache and sadness. I think all of us carry a little of each.

I believe that when you close a door in your life it's best to leave it closed because should you open it again, you never know what or who you're letting back in, and that could be something that affects your life today in a negative way.

It's fine to "revisit the past for a brief time, if only to remember why you left it in the first place," but living in the past steals your present and can affect your future. It keeps you from moving forward, it keeps you stuck in a time in your life that's already passed and it keeps you from living in the moment.

Living in the moment is what leads you into your future.

There are pieces of our past that are meant only for us to remember and sharing that past with the wrong person could be hurtful to them and in the end, to you as well. I'm talking specifically about relationships. The older we get the more of a past we have. We've had past lovers and significant others, heartache, intimate moments, and the doors to those relationships closed when they were over. I've had my share of that as well, yet once those doors were closed I kept them closed. If I were to open those doors of my past then I would be leaving myself vulnerable to what I'm letting back into a life that I had already moved forward from.

Opening the door to a past that was left behind means that you've allowed that energy back or that person back into your life. It means you're choosing to allow the emotions from that time to be felt again, whether good or bad, and it means you're looking at your present life as less important than your past.

We have all those "past" experiences to teach us life lessons so that we can move into a better life and a better relationship. Remembering old loves is a memory to be kept to oneself, at least the intimate details of it. Not everyone feels the way that I do, but I do believe that it can bring hurt knowing too much about your partner's past relationships. There are some pieces of our past that are better left unsaid and kept to ourselves, because living in the past can definitely influence your present life, and that will inevitably can affect your future.

All of us carry some wonderful memories of our past, myself included, but I believe that when we "live" in our past, constantly remembering or talking about our past relationships, then that is a clear sign that we're not happy or content in the relationship we're currently in and that we haven't really gotten over the prior relationship.

Be careful when opening the doors to your past because you never know "what" or "who" you're letting back in and you never know who it's going to hurt.

The past is meant to be left in the past. Your future lies in your present.

Don't lose sight of the people you love in your present life by constantly looking back at the people you left behind in your past.

Be grateful for the people you love in your life today.

After all, you left all the others for a reason.

"Listen To How They Treat You"

"There's a message in the way a person treats you, just listen."

It's that old saying that I absolutely believe in: "actions speak louder than words."

You need the actions to back up the words to make them the truth.

It's about all those loving, positive words that you say to someone that become truth when the actions back them up.

It's true that those negative, hurtful words you say to someone speak the truth about how you feel about them and those words will stay with them for a lifetime.

Ask yourself this: "if you really love someone, be it your significant other, friend, family member or child, why would you say something hurtful to them?" You can't take those words back and if you can say them, then you must have meant them. If you didn't mean them, then why did you say them? Was it to hurt them because you felt you had the right to do so? Was it to push them away or could it be that you said those hurtful words to put them in their place as a way to control them?

You need to stop. You need to stop hurting someone with your words. You need to stop being disrespectful to them with your words. You need to stop trying to control them into submission with your words.

Think about why you say things to hurt someone you love. No human being has the right to hurt another, especially someone who loves you. It could be that you don't really love them, don't understand love, or that love is nothing more than a matter of convenience to you. You must know that each time you say hurtful words to someone you love, you are bruising their heart and that heart begins to shut down little by little. Hurtful words chip away at the heart until it's broken into a million pieces. Yes, I believe that a broken heart can be healed. Let me be clear, it will not be healed by the person that broke it. It can only be healed by the person it was done to.

We're all human and none of us are perfect. There are times we get angry, feel cranky, or have had a bad day. We all have moments like that, but it's NOT okay to hurt someone you love. It's NOT okay to make them feel like your bad mood is their fault because it's not, it's yours and it's NOT okay to think you have the right to say hurtful words to someone because you want to. No human being has the right to hurt another human being.

We have choices in all areas of our life, especially in our relationships. You have a choice of which words you use, the tone of your voice when you say them, and to talk things through calmly instead of being mean and hurtful.

You have a choice to walk away.

Did you have a bad day? Is work getting to you? Are you unhappy? Did someone make you angry or hurt your feelings?

We all rough days now and then, but understand that it's not fair or right to take YOUR rough day out on another.

Think about what you're feeling and try to understand why.

Don't take it out on someone who loves you.

Don't bruise the heart of someone who loves you.

Keep in mind that their feelings are just as important as yours.

Be kind or be quiet.

It's just that simple.

"Leaving Your Light Behind"

We are all beings of light and meet many people along the journey of our life. We share our light and energy with them. We share our life with them. We share our love with them.

When those relationships are over, there are those that leave their light behind and that's not a good thing to do.

Have you ever been in a relationship with someone who was terribly hurt from a prior one?

They left the best part of themselves behind with someone who didn't want them. They brought with them the pain and heartache that someone new doesn't deserve.

There's little left for the person who deserves their love and light.

I never leave my light behind with someone who is no longer in my life. I take my light with me and know that the best is yet to come. The right person will come along and I want to have all my light and good energy to share with them.

When you leave the best part of "you" behind with someone, it prevents you from having a beautiful relationship with the person who deserves it.

You're giving that person the power to prevent you from having a great relationship with the right person when you leave the best part of you behind with someone who didn't want you. Break-ups are difficult, especially when one person didn't want it, but don't compound the pain by bringing that baggage to the next person you're in a relationship with.

There's nothing left to offer the next person who may actually BE the right person. All you choose to bring to someone new is the pain of your past, your heart that isn't fully healed or completely open, and selfish boundaries to make sure that the new person doesn't hurt you.

I was in a relationship in which this wonderful man left his light and the best part of him behind. I spent a few years with him and no matter how good I was to him, he still carried the baggage. He still wouldn't trust me completely. He never opened his whole heart to me. He was afraid to give me all that he had given to the last woman because he felt that I'd do the same thing to him that she had.

It didn't matter how much I loved him or how I proved to him that I wasn't anything like the last girl. It didn't matter that I never broke his trust in me. It didn't matter that I was a different person wanting to be loved in the way that I loved him.

He made a choice to carry the baggage. He made a choice to leave his light behind. He made a choice to leave the best part of himself behind.

His choices were hurtful to me.

I didn't like that he told me I was the "right" girl when he treated me in the "wrong" way.

In time, there was nothing left of me either.

I'm not leaving my light behind. I'm not leaving the best part of me behind. I'm packing all that good stuff up and taking it with me and that is the best "baggage" you can carry along with you into the next relationship.

"Breaking The Love"

Relationships work or they don't. I think that some people are in relationships because they don't want to be alone or that they're comfortable having someone take care of them. The true test of love is how you treat your significant other.

I was in a relationship that was just that. I felt unloved, taken for granted and that my feelings weren't as important theirs. If it wasn't their way then there was no way. If I said "no" because it was best for me it was met with an attitude and hurtful words. I thought it was love because it was love for me, but as time went on I realized that the love I felt for them wasn't the same as their "love" for me.

I began to see the signs of being "unloved." He was happy when he was doing what he wanted to do and was unhappy when things didn't go his way. He was content for me to cook and clean up after him but was annoyed when I asked for help. He was fine as long as I wasn't talking about my feelings and was angry when I did.

I began to notice that he rarely asked me what I wanted to do and almost never asked me how I felt about anything. I began to notice that all his sentences began with "I" and the only ones that began with "you" were when he was telling me what was wrong with me. I began to notice that all the things that I did for him were expected, not appreciated, and when I wasn't able to do them, he was angry.

He broke my love for him. He broke all those wonderful feelings I had for him, that overwhelming "I can't believe I finally met the right person" feeling, that "I can't wait for him to get home from work because I miss him" feeling, and that "be still my heart, he sent me a romantic text" feeling.

He broke my love for him. He broke us. He broke the possibilities of a life together. He broke the trust I had in him to keep my heart safe. He broke my self-esteem of thinking I was enough for him and realizing that I wasn't enough at all. He broke my ability to love this life we were building to one of anxiety at the thought of upsetting him. He broke a girl who thought she was seen by him for all the good things that he said she was, only to become a girl who was now invisible to him.

He broke the love, but he didn't break me.

He may have broken a lot, but he didn't break me.

He broke everything else.

I never needed him, but he needed me.

I always wanted him, but he never wanted me.

I gave him all of me and he gave me what was left of him from the others before me.

I gave him love and light, he gave me pain and darkness.

I was vulnerable with my heart and feelings with him and he used that vulnerability to hurt me.

I took back "ME" and won't be giving myself away again so freely to someone who doesn't deserve me.

He may have broken the love but he didn't break the dream that real love exists.

Sometimes everything has to be broken so that we can put it back together even stronger.

"Broken Hearts Will Heal"

We've all had our hearts broken at one time or another in our life and if there's one thing I've learned, it's this: it doesn't suddenly break. It takes time to break it.

It's breaks because someone has been chipping away at it over and over again.

When most of the heart has been chipped away, there's not much left to hold it together until one day it breaks altogether.

It can be repaired but it will never be the same heart that it once was. Only the broken hearted can heal their heart and in time, it will heal and be stronger than the heart that had been broken.

There's all types of abuse out there, yet nothing will chip away at a heart more than verbal and emotional abuse. Those are the worst and I know this for a fact because I've been the person on the other side of it more times than I can count. It's a difficult and long process to heal from, but it is possible because I've done it.

I'm going to be honest about this subject because I can speak from personal experience.

Words and actions hurt. They chip away at a heart that loves someone so much that they allow it to happen, at least until the day that they've had enough. It happens when that person gets stronger and begins the process of rebuilding a heart that's been broken into a million pieces.

That is the day that they've had enough.

It's the day they've seen the truth of the person who treats them that way.

It's the day that they realize their value and make a decision that they will no longer allow that behavior.

No one deserves to be treated badly, even the ones who treat others badly.

Love doesn't hurt the heart. Abusive words and behaviors do.

There are some who don't realize just how hurtful their words and actions can be to someone they love, especially when that person still loves them and sees the good in them. The day will come after countless conversations between two people that they realize just how much damage they have done.

It's the day the heart breaks after being chipped away at over and over again.

The good news is that a heart that breaks is proof that it works. It's proof that you have a heart that truly knows how to love someone.

Hearts that have been chipped at over time will eventually break, but they also will be given the chance to heal into a stronger heart, one which won't settle for less than it deserves.

We are all in control of how we treat others.

We are all in control of our feelings.

We are all in control of healing our hearts, knowing our value, and accepting nothing less than what we deserve.

CHAPTER EIGHT

"A Breath About Family"

"One Chair"

I will always remember my grandmothers' reaction whenever she saw a two seater car. It seems like a lifetime ago, yet to this day I remember her response. She'd say: "That's a selfish car. There's only enough room for two people." It was a funny thing to hear her say, yet as I've grown older, I began to understand what she meant by that.

I'm that way with chairs.

My front porch has two chairs on one side of the door and a table and two chairs on the other. I'm usually in one of those chairs throughout the day and evening and look forward to the people I love sitting with me in the other chair.

There's not always someone sitting with me but there's always a chair just waiting for someone who needs to use it.

When I see someone put only one chair out for themselves it makes a statement. It tells me that they want to be alone or that they don't want me sitting with them at all. It tells me that they never gave a thought about how I was feeling and that I may be feeling the need for someone to give me a chair.

Sometimes we all need a chair. We need that second chair to know we're not alone. We need that second chair so that we don't feel lonely. We need that second chair to let us know that someone is just waiting for us to sit in it and spend time with us.

The second chair lets us know that someone wants us.

The second chair lets us know that someone loves us.

The second chair lets us know that we matter.

Whenever I see only one chair, I see a person who is selfish, who doesn't care about anyone other than themselves and a person who takes the people in their life for granted.

You can choose to spend your life with only one chair, but keep in mind what that one chair may represent to those that love and care about you.

Remember, a day may come in which there won't be a person to fill that second chair and you'll be sitting there alone.

I love having two chairs on my front porch.

It's my small way of letting the people I love and care about know that they're always welcome to be with me, that they are loved, and that spending time with them is precious to me.

Chairs.

How many do you have?

I hope you have more than one.

"A Flood Of Memories"

Isn't it funny how one random moment in your day can bring back a flood of emotions from a moment in your past? I had such a moment and for just an hour or so it allowed a literal flood of pain and heartache from my past to revisit me.

I want to share it with you because if there's one thing I've learned, it's this: when I write from the heart and share my most intimate emotions with you, it's therapeutic for me. It takes those emotions out of my soul and puts them onto paper and it's truly a good thing for me. I hope it's a good thing for those of you going through a similar situation.

It was a day that the Jersey Shore was hit with a tremendous amount of rain which caused massive flooding in our surrounding areas. There were those that needed to be taken from their homes and cars by boat. I didn't go through anything that extreme but what I had gone through was heartbreaking to me.

The rain had hit hard in the morning and around 11 am my son, Noah, went down into our basement. I heard him say "Mom, you better get down here."

My heart sank because I knew it wasn't going to be good and I was right. My basement was flooded. I went down the stairs and looked around. There was water everywhere and all I could focus on was the cardboard boxes that were filled with their favorite childhood books and memories that were now completely soaked in water. I knew right then and there that we had lost all of those things that we all felt were "important." Water was everywhere and I was overwhelmed wondering where to begin.

Yet, I knew in my heart where to begin and it was to begin throwing things out.

The task of cleaning up had begun. It was hours and hours that my youngest, Sam, and I filled one garbage bag after another with their childhood memories: books, papers, toys, stuffed animals and more. I began to think back to another time in my life when I was going through another time of throwing my "memories" in the trash.

It was over 7 years ago that I was getting out of a second marriage that never should have happened. At that time I had lost the house I designed, built and lived in for over 20 years. I lost my home, my car, and all the money the kids and I had saved up over the years. I remember two dumpsters in my driveway for two weeks as the kids and I threw out as much as we could, knowing that we were moving to a much smaller house.

I can remember the heartache of throwing out things that had meant so much to me and to them, but we didn't have much choice. The home we lived in was so much larger than the home we were moving to and still live in. I had to keep telling myself that it was just "stuff" and that I could take the memories with me.

It was a painful time to lose literally everything we had, but we did it and we moved into our "Cozy Cottage."

We were fine. We were happy. We were grateful.

I moved to this new place with nothing. I had no car, no money and no job, yet we had each other and within a few weeks I had another car, some money, and a job.

I've been rebuilding my life ever since.

The flood in the basement of our "Cozy Cottage" brought back all those emotions I felt from seven years ago. I'll admit that I shed a few tears as I filled garbage bag after garbage bag with more memories. It was painful and overwhelming, but I kept filling bags with their favorite children's books to stuffed animals, one right after another, and Sam kept bringing them up the stairs and out the door to the trash. It wasn't the exact "Mother/Son" day I would have planned, but we did it together. It took us days to finish the task, but I was grateful when it was done.

I reminded myself that these things were possessions, just the "stuff" that we had compiled for many years. Throwing the stuff out didn't erase the memories, it just got rid of the physical stuff. We'll always have the memories of that favorite book or stuffed animal.

We'll always carry the memories in our hearts.

Sometimes we need to be reminded of the things that we had tried to forget because we shouldn't forget anything, we should learn from it, accept it and move forward.

After all, we don't lose the precious moments we have of our children or loved ones. They are embedded into our minds and hearts forever. The physical possession is a wonderful thing to have but losing it doesn't erase what our heart holds deep inside.

Our hearts take pictures of those moments in life that mean the most and no flood, no fire, and no one person can ever take that away.

It was a "flood of memories" that reminded me, not of what we had lost, but of how much we have.

"Feels Like Family Again"

Two of my five children live at home, so there are moments I feel the pang of the "empty nest" syndrome. I've gotten used to my three oldest living across the country, only seeing them every year or two, so I don't feel that pain of missing them all living home very often. They've been living out of my home for years now and I'm used to my two youngest being the only ones here with me.

Then, I had a day in which it felt like the old days and I was reminded of just how much I miss having a house filled with five children.

My oldest son, Eric, flew in from the West Coast and it must have been close to two years since I'd seen him. He brought his beautiful girl, Sophia, home with him for all of us to meet and she was amazing! We fell in love with her instantly and I'd like to believe that she felt the same about us.

I raced to the airport early that day to pick them up and the moment I saw my son the tears began to fall. They both walked towards me with open arms, hugs, kisses and some amazing West Coast energy! It was just what this mom needed!

Seeing him was so much more than a hug. It brought back a wealth of emotions and memories of having them all live at home together. I remembered family dinners at the table every night and weekends filled with a stream of teenagers coming in and out of the house and hanging around. It was heaven.

This day felt like old times for me. I watched him as he laughed with his two youngest brothers and saw such pride and happiness in his face as he introduced them to his girl. I can remember feeling such a sense of peace, happiness and pure joy.

I had forgotten what it was like to have my family together like that. These days even my two youngest are working or going to school and I feel as though they've already left the nest.

That day felt like old times, even though two of my kids were missing. It felt like the family I remembered which had turned into the family that grew up and moved on to their own adult lives. I remembered all those precious memories yet was also watching them make new ones together. Suddenly, the babies and teenagers I remembered were sitting at a restaurant out to dinner with me but they were grown up! They had become men in what felt like an instant.

My four boys have grown up into amazing men, and I don't say that just because I'm their mom.

They are respectful, kind, compassionate and non-judgmental. They are truly the type of people I had hoped and wished that they would grow up to be and they are.

I sat in amazement that night at dinner, savoring every moment, taking in all that surrounded me. It was a night I'll remember forever, until the next time we can all be together to make new memories.

I felt so much pride for these boys that night, especially my oldest. I watched how he spoke to and treated his girl. He loves her, she loves him, and the respect they have for one another is the type that a mother hopes her child will find in a partner.

I'm so happy that he found that.

It was an incredible night of being a family together again.

It was a night of my heart being so filled with love that it could have exploded.

These boys of mine are a gift to the world.

They have been and always will be a gift to me.

I'll always remember that wonderful night when it felt like family again.

"Hey 17"

Every so often I have a week filled with one wonderful thing after another, not just as a writer, but as a mom. I had such a week in September of 2018. The youngest of my five children, Sam, bought his first car with the money he earned from his job, passed his road test and got his driver's license, began his senior year of high school and first year of vocational school for carpentry. So many wonderful milestones in just one week, and as his mom, it's been a week of mixed emotions. I've felt happiness, joy and excitement yet in the midst of all these great feelings there was a twinge of it all feeling bittersweet.

After all, this is my baby, my youngest of five, and the moment of truth hit me hard that this really is the last of my children to graduate high school. Once he graduates in June there will be no more "first day" of school pictures, no more shopping for school supplies, no more shopping for school clothes. There will be no more envelopes stuffed with school forms to be filled out or a table scattered with books that need to be covered. There will be no more packing lunches or making sure that they don't miss the bus. It's a chapter that will soon be closed and I'm not quite sure how a parent prepares themselves for that day.

I have five kids worth of 12 years of first day of school pictures.

I have five kids who got their driver's license in 12 years.

I've attended four kids high school graduations with one more to go.

Therein lies the bittersweet.

The happiness and excitement was seeing the expression on my son's face as the driving instructor told him he passed his driving test and that look continued as we went into the office to get his license. He was so happy to have his license in his hand. To him it meant a new chapter in his life and at 17 years old, it meant freedom.

We came home and he threw his surfboard into the car that he had just bought and drove to the beach. It was the first time that he drove alone and it brought me back to the day I got my driver's license. I remembered all those feelings of how I felt when I drove by myself for the first time. I knew exactly how he was feeling because I had once felt the same.

So many "firsts" in the lives of my five children mixed in with so many "lasts."

I hold all the memories of their "firsts" deep within my heart and I hold the "lasts" there as well. After all, life is filled with endings and new beginnings.

As far as my children are concerned, they still have so many "firsts" that have yet to happen and I look forward to being a part of each and every one of them.

"The Last Child"

The youngest of my five children graduated high school last week. It was a bittersweet day for both of us, yet an exciting one. It was the end of one chapter and the beginning of a new one for both of us, but his chapter is much different than mine. It's a new beginning for both of us.

This fifth child of mine never ceases to amaze me. At just 17 years old (almost 18) he knows who he is, he's comfortable in his own skin, and he doesn't care what anyone thinks of him. I don't remember being that self-confident at that age and I think most adults still struggle with being themselves even as we grow older.

I'm a mother who is blessed to witness just how much he is loved and respected by others for being his authentic self. I can't begin to tell you how many teachers, faculty members and parents of his friends tell me what a sweet kid he is. He's kind, respectful and funny. The women who work in the high school office have told me that he always makes time to stop by and say "hi" to them, ask how they are and that he always leaves there giving them a complement and telling them to have a wonderful day. No mother could ask for anything more or feel more proud!

I can't help but think back to when I was that age and wasn't even close to being sure of myself. I didn't know what I wanted in life other than the next step after high school: go to college. I cared about what I was wearing and what others thought of me. I wanted to fit in with the crowd and sit at the "cool kids" lunch table. Comfortable in my own skin? I didn't even know what my "own skin" was. Did I feel confident of who I was then? I don't know of many of my classmates that were "confident" with who they were because we were still trying to figure out who we were.

Yes, I'm a proud mother and one that is in awe of this fifth child of mine, yet I'll be honest, I feel the same way about all five of my children. They are who they are and they're amazing human beings. I'd like to think I had a hand in that while I was raising them because I allowed them the freedom to be their authentic self, without judgment or criticism, and I'd have to say it worked.

All five of them are different in their own way and I love them even more for that. They're compassionate, respectful, and most importantly, they are KIND to everyone, whether they know them or not. They're willing to help someone without expecting anything in return and they're doing what they can to make this world a better place.

We all want to be accepted and loved and I believe that happens when we are our "authentic self," not someone other people expect us to be. As I told my children, if people don't like you or respect you for who you are, then they're not your "people."

It's a lesson I learn more and more as life goes on.

I believe that the world is a better place because of my five children.

I believe that the world is a better place for all of us that are trying to make it that way.

Here's to all of us being our authentic self and beginning another chapter in our lives.

Enjoy the journey and embrace the adventure.

"MY NEPHEW, GAVIN"

"A dreamer is a realist with faith."

It's having faith in their dreams and faith in themselves.

I traveled to Virginia this year to celebrate my nephew, Gavin's, high school graduation. It was the first time in years that so much of our family was under the same roof for the night and to say that we had a good time would be an understatement. We reconnected with one another, catching up on what each of us was doing in our lives, and we laughed. My goodness, we laughed!

I was lucky enough to spend some alone time with my nephew, Gavin. We had a conversation I'll remember forever: he shared his "dreams" with me.

We spoke of college and his football career, but most of the conversation was about his dreams.

He said he must get that "dreamer" thing from me.

I couldn't have felt more proud.

Gavin told me that he wants to make a difference in the world, even if it's making a difference to just one person. He told me that he's not looking to be famous, but if he is he wants to be famous for helping people and changing someone's life for the better. He told me his "dreams" of a better world and I understood exactly what he was talking about because I dream of the same. Gavin and I aren't just waiting for our dreams to come true, we're doing what it takes to turn our dreams into a reality.

I received a "thank you" card from Gavin a few weeks after his party and this proud auntie shed a tear at the last line of the card: "We're dreamers together 'til the end!"

We will always will be.

I believe in the "dreamers" because I've been one for as long as I can remember. When I was much younger I remember being told that it was okay to have dreams as long as I understood that they were just dreams, not reality. I used to believe that a dreamer was just a person who went through life with their head in the clouds, but that's not true.

We dreamers have our feet planted firmly on the ground, yet we have enough faith in ourselves to believe that we can turn our dreams into reality. We have an intense passion for our dreams and we believe in our dreams and in ourselves.

I believe in my nephew with all of my heart. I believe that he will turn his dreams into reality. I believe that he will make a difference in the world and in the life of another.

I believe this because he's made a difference in mine.

Thank you, Gavin, for letting your aunt know that she made a difference in your life and thank you for making a difference in mine.

Believe in yourself. Believe in your dreams. Believe that you can make a difference in the world.

After all, that's what us "dreamers" are all about.

"My Thanksgiving Table"

Thanksgiving is my favorite holiday. There's no stress of buying and wrapping gifts or decorating the house and a tree. It's a day to prepare a feast for family and loved ones and a day to set your "Thanksgiving Table." It's a day to relax and enjoy the people around your table with no strings attached.

I begin my Thanksgiving preparations the day before. I bake a few pies, chop vegetables for my crudite platter and make homemade cranberry sauce. I make onion and veggie dip and set my table.

I never know how many people will be around my table. Three of my children are scattered across the country and aren't always able to fly home. There's also loved ones that have passed who will be there in spirit."

It's at this time of year that I think of the "Thanksgiving Tables" of the years gone by.

I remember a time when there were more than 15 people around my table, and all the many others that filled the house after dinner for dessert. It was filled with my aunts and uncles, cousins, parents, my grandmother and children. It was a time of sitting together and watching old home movies, listening to stories of the older generation and memories of running around the house with the cousins.

Children grow up and move out on their own and loved ones get older and pass away. Each year there seems to be one more person missing from the table.

Each year as I sit down at my "Thanksgiving Table," I will remember the days of holidays past and I will remember the loved ones that I lost. I will remember the laughter and the stories they told, the expressions of their faces and the warmth of their embrace. I will remember their colorful personalities and their presence and importance in the family. I will remember the days when all of us young ones were sitting at the "kid's table" until we reached the important age of sitting at the "big table." It was a rite of passage to graduate to that table.

My brother used to say "I wonder who will be missing from the table next year." I always thought that was a terrible thing to say, but he was right and it taught me to embrace each holiday and each day with the people in my life because life is truly short. I'm learning that lesson more and more as I get older. I don't look at the table and wonder which chair will be empty next year but look at the table filled with the blessings of family, love, and laughter. It's a day of making memories and we carry those memories in our hearts forever. We may lose a loved one, but we can never lose the memories of them.

I know that each year I'll be missing someone at my table each year, yet I'll be seeing the "Thanksgiving Tables" of my past and the people that once surrounded it. They may not all be sitting around it, but their spirit will be around it forever and for that, I will be grateful.

"Twas the Morning Of Christmas"

'Twas the morning of Christmas and all through our home
Everyone was sleeping and I was alone
With a hot cup of coffee and my pup at my feet,
I turned on my laptop and sat in my seat.
The kids were still snuggled and sleeping in bed
But visions of past Christmases danced in my head.
I remembered when they were younger and so very small
And waited for Santa and his reindeer to call.
Then all of a sudden I knew what was the matter
I was afraid the magic of Christmas had become shattered
'Fore as we grow older we tend to forget
That Christmas is much more than the presents we get
It's remembering the magic and beauty of the season
After all, Christmastime was born with a reason.
So I say to you all take a moment to remember
To believe in the magic in this month of December
It's time to stop writing, I see children in sight,
Merry Christmas to all and to all love and light.

"New Year's Eve"

I sit here with my thoughts on New Year's Eve
Wondering what I will take and what I will leave
It's a brand new year, no mistakes in it yet
Filled with hopes and dreams still waiting to be met.

I've learned many lessons from the year that has passed
I've let go of some things that weren't meant to last
I'm taking those lessons with me as I move on ahead
Negativity and drama are two burdens I will shed.

It's all up from here with this new year in sight,
It's time to bring to it my love and my light,
It's time to make a difference in the life of another
It's time to spread kindness to all of the other's.

It's time for dreaming, to hold onto the faith
That all things are possible, they're just lying in wait
For us to grab onto them and do what we can
To make our life better and lend the world a helping hand.

So here's to the New Year all shiny and new,
Here's to all the great things that I know we can do.
Take all your lessons and the people you hold dear
And make this the most amazing of all your New Year's.

"The New Year's Revelations"

I write about this subject in one form or another every year, and this year is no exception.

Every year I notice that as the New Year approaches, people start talking about their "resolutions." There's things they want to do and things they want to change in their life so they make a list of "resolutions."

I threw that concept out years ago because to me, resolutions were nothing more than making promises to myself that I couldn't keep. They were goals for sure, but seriously, how many of us actually stick to those resolutions? I always tried, failed at some, then beat myself up for not doing what I had wanted.

So, years ago I realized that the only way for my life to change was by learning the lessons that life had handed me, by learning from my mistakes, learning from my experiences, and so I decided to have my "New Year's Revelations!"

I ask myself some important questions throughout the month of December: What opened my eyes this past year? What did I learn about myself? What type of people are in my bubble? Am I taking care of myself and loving myself enough or giving too much of myself away? What do I need to let go of that has no place in the New Year coming up and in my life?

These are the questions to ask yourself and answer honestly. You see, when you have those "revelations" about yourself and the year that's about to come to an end, you take those lessons and truths with you. You begin the New Year with a better understanding of yourself, your life, your situations and the people in it. When you do that, the New Year will bring all that you want it to: love, happiness, joy, adventure, new beginnings, and new opportunities. The possibilities are endless.

Don't put added stress on yourself by making "resolutions."

Take the time to think about your "revelations" and begin the New Year in a positive light.

All things are possible if you just believe in yourself!

Happy New Year! Happy New You!

CHAPTER NINE

"A Breath About Good Things"

"It's A Good Thing"

I believe that "it's a good thing" to think positive thoughts, surround yourself with positive people, and be grateful for each day that you wake up in the morning. It's a great practice to begin each day with gratitude and to end each day by counting your blessings.

Life is what you make it and I hope that you make your life amazing, because each one of us has something to bring to the world and the people in it.

Here's some random thoughts that so often cross my mind and help to remind me to stay on a positive path.

I am loved.

I am grateful for being gifted another day to live my best life.

I am grateful for all the blessings in my life.

Be kind and spread kindness everywhere you go.

Each new day is filled with endless possibilities and a chance to do it better than the day before.

My eyes and my heart are open to see the beauty that surrounds me.

I choose to let go of the past so that the doors to my future can open.

Love yourself in the way that you want to be loved because you can't expect someone else to do what you can't do for yourself.

Kindness can heal the world.

You can't change others, but you can change yourself.

Be self-less.

Be your authentic self.

Fill your bubble with positive people.

Always stand in your truth.

Choose your words carefully because they will never be forgotten.

Love your life and it will love you back.

Joy is an elevated state of happiness.

Say "no" if you need to and remember that "no" is a full sentence.

You can enable bad behavior or disable your control over it.

Take care of yourself as much as you take care of others.

Don't settle for less than you deserve.

Trust is earned and must be maintained.

Dream as big as you can.

Dreamers are the ones brave enough to go out into the world and turn them into a reality.

Be brave at every chance you get.

Everything begins with YOU!

Love someone for who they are, not for who you want them to be.

No one's feelings are wrong.

Always be considerate.

Speak positively to others and to yourself.

Don't keep looking back in your life, look forward.

Pay attention to what's in front of you because what's behind you is over.

Be mindful.

Always encourage, never discourage.

Sometimes you have to love someone enough to let them go.

Everything happens as it should, how it should, and when it should.

You're of no use to anyone unless you love yourself first.

First and foremost, find your funny.

Laugh as often as you can.

Music soothes the soul.

Dance when no one and everyone is looking.

Projection is the inability to take accountability.

Mean people do exist but you don't have to be one of them.

Don't be afraid to show the world who you are.

Don't judge people.

The right people want everything FOR you while the wrong people want everything FROM you.

Stop caring about what other people think about you.

Count your blessings as often as you can.

"Down days" happen to remind us of all the "good days" we have.

Always be open to a new adventure.

Always listen to your intuition. If it's telling you that something is wrong, trust that it is.

Intuition never lies.

Believe in yourself even when no one else does.

Find peace in your life.

Be brave enough to say "I'm sorry" to someone you've hurt.

Don't be a victim to traumatic experiences in your life. Be a survivor of them.

Words can be beautiful and heartfelt but they're only true if you have the actions to back them up.

Communication is the key to everything.

Set healthy boundaries for yourself and don't let anyone cross them.

You have to brush off the dust that life leaves on you in order to see the light.

Make the time to have some fun.

Tell someone what you love about them.

Don't take anyone for granted.

Know what's important in your life and what isn't.

Don't let yourself get caught up in the drama of someone else because it belongs to them, not you.

If someone causes you stress, wish them love and light and let them go.

Be the person who will give your time and attention to someone that needs it.

You have the ability to make someone happy.

Do at least one thing everyday that makes you feel good.

Write a love note to someone you love.

Let the people you love and care for know when you're thinking of them. Send a text, a message or give them a call. You'll make their day and yours.

Spend time under the full moon.

Wake up early and watch the sunrise.

Enjoy a sunset with someone you love and care about.

Lay on the grass and stare at the stars.

Go to the beach and soak in the sounds and smells of the ocean.

Sit outside in the sun and soak in its' healing rays.

Bake cookies and eat them warm.

Enjoy a meal around the table with people you care about.

Cook so that everyone can "taste the love."

Take a walk when it's snowing.

Stand in the rain and let it wash over you.

Keep yourself grounded by walking barefoot on the grass.

Drink iced water with lemon.

Read a good book with your favorite cup of tea.

Keep a journal and look back at it a year later to see how far you've come and how much you've grown.

Embrace every piece of your life.

Hug someone for a minute and feel the love.

Give someone flowers "just because."

Do random acts of kindness every single day.

Learn to love "Mercury in Retrograde."

Make love because you want to.

Call an old friend or family member.

Plan a romantic night for the one you love.

Take a break from the world. Shut off the television, computer and cell phone and just "be."

Be empathetic to others.

Don't lose sight of the people in your life.

Make promises you can keep.

Be respectful of the feelings of others.

Be quick to admit when you're wrong and don't brag when you're right.

Be a free spirit.

Everything and anything is possible if you believe it is.

Life is about taking a leap of faith.

Teach someone something and learn something new.

Watch your favorite movie on a rainy day.

Always say "please and thank you."

Donate what you don't need to someone who needs it.

Always keep a sense of humor.

Put your favorite quote where you can see it everyday.

Never forget the people who helped you along the way.

It's okay to want to spend time alone.

Spend time with family and friends.

Take a long hot lavender bath, light some candles and play your favorite music.

Love as long as you can and as hard as you can.

Do what's best for your soul.

Kiss the one you love a lot.

Don't listen to gossip.

Be open minded, not small minded.

Don't hold a grudge.

Forgive the people who hurt you, but do it for YOU, not THEM. It's the only way to let go of the anger you feel.

We all make mistakes. Forgive yourself for them.

A good cry is sometimes all you need to feel better. Let the tears flow.

Don't give away your power.

Don't leave your light and the best part of you with the last person you were in a relationship with.

You always have a choice.

We don't become who we are by "chance," we become who we are by "choice."

Don't lie.

You matter.

You are important.

Someone in this world couldn't imagine life without you.

One person may not be able to change the world alone, but together we can try.

"It's a good thing."

On A Final Note...

Thank you to all of you who purchased "Each Breath Along The Journey." I hope you enjoy it as much as I enjoyed writing it.

Life isn't always easy for any of us, yet my hope is that by sharing my intimate and personal experiences with you, you'll know you're not alone. I believe that we are all connected in one way or another, and that the more we stand in our truth and share our experiences with each other, the more we can make a positive difference in each others lives.

In fact, I truly believe that together we can make a difference in this world and what a wonderful world it would be.

Life isn't perfect, yet always believe that your life is perfect for you.

Love yourself.

Be kind to others.

Live the best life you can and make each day count.

It's a good thing.

Wishing you love and light,

~Anne Dennish~